GREAT LAKES MARITIME HISTORY:
BIBLIOGRAPHY AND
SOURCES OF INFORMATION

by
Dr. Charles E. Feltner
and
Jeri Baron Feltner

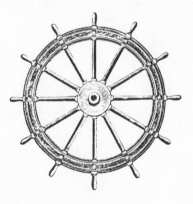

FIRST EDITION
December 1982

SEAJAY PUBLICATIONS
P.O. Box 2176
Dearborn, MI 48123

DEDICATION

To Derek, Doug, Eddie, Kay and Mark

Library of Congress Catalog Card Number 82-051175

Copyright 1982 by Seajay Publications

First Edition, First Printing 1982

Printed in the United States of America

ISBN 0-9609014-0-X

Published by Seajay Publications, P.O. Box 2176, Dearborn, MI 48123

"Knowledge is of two kinds. We know a subject ourselves, or we know where we can find information upon it."

Boswell, "Life of Johnson," 1775

The fore-and-aft Schooner BURT BARNES under full sail. This type of vessel and rig is the quintessence of the history of transportation on the Great Lakes. *(Photo courtesy Walter Hirthe)*

TABLE OF CONTENTS

⚓

FOREWORD

It has been observed that a great deal of America's most exciting history unfolded in the region of the Great Lakes, and yet much of it remains to this day unresearched and unwritten. The broad patterns of the region's past have been documented by such authors as Parkman, Mansfield, Curwood and Havighurst, and a host of popular writers like Bowen, Boyer, Ratigan and Hatcher have brought back to life for modern readers the more memorable incidents along the way. Much, however, still cries out for discovery. Thousands of thrilling stories are hidden in the yellowed pages of old newspapers, veritable legions of men and women who shaped our past are yet to be recognized, and painfully little is understood about the technology of historic Lakes' ships. There is much to be done!

Those who are well schooled in historical studies know that there are incredibly rich resources available with which the Lakes' unexpressed history may be reconstructed, but it is not just the trained historian who has written the region's story. Instead, a large part of that task has fallen to hobbyists and amateur historians, who, in general, know little of the sources or the methodology for efficient research. A surprising amount of what we know about the Lakes, the ships, and the men who sailed them, is published in newsletters and journals whose contributors have few credentials, and yet, with casual, almost accidental technique, many have been able to produce very valid and important work.

The authors, Charles and Jeri Baron Feltner, became interested in Great Lakes maritime history in 1977, and soon afterward began researching shipwrecks around the Straits of Mackinac. They earned distinction rapidly because of their fine work. Together they possessed strong background and training in research methods, and shared a sense of purpose. They conducted laborious research, located and filmed several virgin shipwrecks, dove a wide variety of wrecksites, churned out an impressive list of fine articles on the subject, lectured all over the Great Lakes States as well as Canada, and contributed substantially to the control and preservation of our shipwreck resources. In recognition of the scarcity of research tools for students and scholars of Great Lakes history, they also took the initiative to develop and put into print a study methodology. The present bibliography and source guide is the result.

This compendium is the product of several years of painstaking work in archives, libraries, and private collections all over the Midwest and Canada. It identifies a wide variety of source materials related to maritime history in the Great Lakes region, and guides the researcher to more general marine references as well. A number of useful bibliographies have been published previously, but none has approached the scope of the Feltner list, nor come near satisfying the needs of the untrained student. This book brings to every researcher the capability of locating the best information, no matter how unsophisticated the library facilities in their community nor how inexperienced the researchers themselves. It has taken the mystery out of the process and so simplified it that any serious layman becomes capable of undertaking productive research.

Several publications have become basic tools for Great Lakes studies. Mansfield's ambitious *History of the Great Lakes*, published in 1899, is still the most utilized single source of information on the subject. The annual *List of Merchant Vessels of the United States* (known as "Merchant Vessels") is an exceptional source of historical data. William Lytle's *Merchant Steam Vessels of the United States, 1790-1868* (the "Lytle List"), and John Mills' *Canadian Coastal and Inland Steam Vessels, 1809-1930* (the "Mills List") were monumental contributions. The "Feltner Bibliography" undoubtedly will fill a similar niche on the bookshelves of both the casual and the serious student. That it will simplify the work of the researcher there can be little doubt. It is hoped that it will also stimulate others to take up the unfinished business of piecing together the rich and inspiring history of the Inland Seas, about which there is so very much yet to tell.

C. *Patrick Labadie*
Duluth, Minnesota
November 18, 1982

PREFACE

This bibliography was originally compiled because we needed it for a course we were teaching on "How to Research Great Lakes Ships and Shipwrecks." No other comparable document existed. Several limited scope bibliographies on Great Lakes maritime matters have been written (and some have been published). This bibliography, though much more comprehensive than others (it contains over 1,000 citations), is not exhaustive and still contains some shortcomings (see Appendix entitled "Perspectives"). Nevertheless, we believe it serves a very useful purpose for those interested in the subject matter. Although much remains to be done, we have gone forward with publication. We feel supported in our decision by Sir Winston Churchill who advised, *"I contend my friend, it is better to do something, rather than nothing, while waiting to do everything."* This document represents an effort on our part to *"do something"* to advance the state of the aggregation and organization of printed knowledge about Great Lakes Maritime History.

Chuck & Jeri Feltner
Dearborn, Michigan
December 17, 1982

GEO. B. CARPENTER & CO.

Ship Chandlers

Sail Makers

202-208 S. Water St., cor. 5th Ave., Chicago.

GALVANIZED IRON WIRE ROPE

For Standing Rigging.

STANDARD LIFE PRESERVERS.

SPIRIT COMPASSES

All Sizes—Get the Best!

ANCHORS
BLOCKS
CHAINS
TAR
PITCH
OAKUM
PAINTS
OILS.

FLAGS

Cotton Duck,

ALL WIDTHS,

And everything belonging
to such a stock.

JOSEPH GRAY,

DEALER IN ALL KINDS OF

TOBACCO, CIGARS, PIPES and STATIONERY.

No. 9 West Randolph Street, Chicago.

Marine Record, Barnet's Coast Pilot and Marine Law Books on sale.

(Reprinted from *Barnet's Coast Pilot*)

ACKNOWLEDGEMENT

In preparing this bibliography, we came in contact with a large number of people in libraries, historical societies, museums, governmental agencies and private homes who provided information and guidance. All whom we approached were sympathetic to the project we had undertaken and gave generously of their time. For this we are indeed grateful and would like to express our appreciation to all those who assisted in this project. Several deserve special mention.

Our greatest debt is owed to DR. WALTER HIRTHE of Milwaukee, Wisconsin. He originally helped coax us into the field of Great Lakes maritime history and has assiduously pursued the task of being our mentor and inspiration. At every juncture he has gone out of his way to unselfishly help us. In the publication of this bibliography, we sincerely hope that Wally enjoys seeing a harvest reaped for which he helped plant and nurture some of the seeds.

C. PATRICK LABADIE, Curator of the Canal Park Marine Museum in Duluth, Minnesota, contributed substantially to our work by providing numerous citations which we have included in this publication. Pat has always been more than generous with the information he holds. On a technical basis, he has contributed more overall to the value of this bibliography than anyone else. Moreover, he has always held a very deep conviction that a work of this type should be produced. For these reasons we asked him to write the *Foreword*.

KEN HALL of the U.S. National Archives and Records Service in Washington, D.C., reviewed the manuscript in-depth and provided numerous suggestions concerning the citation of material available from NARS. Ken originally lived in Wyandotte, Michigan, and throughout his many years with NARS he has maintained his interest and expertise in Great Lakes maritime history. His contributions to this publication have been invaluable.

DR. RICHARD WRIGHT, Director of the Center for Archival Collections at Bowling Green State University in Ohio, provided comments which helped set the overall tone of this manuscript. GREGORY GREGORY, formerly of the Marine Room of the Milwaukee Public Library in Wisconsin, cheerfully guided us to a number of the citations that we have included. MAURICE SMITH, Director of the Marine Museum at Kingston (Ontario), kindly provided us with a copy of the unpublished bibliography on Canadian sources. O.O. "STRETCH" LILJEQUIST and PAUL WOEHRMANN of the Milwaukee Public Library helped us on numerous occasions in accessing material. ALICE DALLIGAN, Chief of the Burton Historical Collection of the Detroit Public Library, reviewed the manuscript and provided some pointers. MICHAEL KNES, also of the Burton Historical Collection, was always available to help with special problems. THOM HOLDEN of the Canal Park Marine Museum in Duluth sent us copies of several important citations. We greatly appreciate the contributions of these people.

Substantial cooperation and help was received from all of the major libraries and maritime organizations around the Great Lakes. To enumerate them all would virtually repeat Section 12 of this bibliography. Several individuals not already mentioned in these institutions deserve recognition. They include: JANET COE SANBORN, Editor of Inland Seas in Cleveland; JOHN POLASCEK, Curator of the Dossin Marine Museum in Detroit; FRANK CREVIER and TED RICHARDSON of the Museum of Arts and History in Port Huron; JIM MINTON, LUCY COHEN and JOHN GANNT of the University of Michigan Library in Ann Arbor, and NANCY LEVEY of the Henry Ford Centennial Library in Dearborn, Michigan.

Several private individuals have helped us in a variety of ways. Some of them, but certainly not all, are PAUL ACKERMAN, LARRY BARON, DICK and NANCY CAMPBELL, DICK CHARBONNEAU, BEN CLINE, EDNA COFFMAN (deceased), DAVID DONOVAN, PAUL HORN, MIKE KOHUT, ED PUSICK, DICK RACE, MARY BELLE SHURTLEFF, JOHN STEELE and KEN TEYSEN.

In closing, we offer a very special and warm thank you to those mentioned and a host of others too numerous to mention who have contributed their capable assistance and encouragement. Without all of you our task would have been well-nigh impossible.

Chuck and Jeri Feltner

1-A.   BASIC RESEARCH TOOLS

Cheney, Frances Neel, and Williams, Wiley J. Fundamental Reference
    Sources. 2nd ed. Chicago: American Library Association, 1980.

Downs, Robert B. How To Do Library Research. Urbana: University of
    Illinois Press, 1966.

Higgens, Gavin, ed. Printed Reference Material. London: The Library
    Association, 1980.

Sheehy, Eugene P. Guide to Reference Books. 9th ed. Chicago: American
    Library Association, 1976.

Vitale, Philip H. Basic Tools of Research. Woodbury, New York: Barron's
    Educational Series, 1968.

Walford, A. J. Guide to Reference Material. 3rd ed. 3 vols. London: The
    Library Association, 1973-77. (In progress 4th ed. v. 1-, 1980-.)

1-B.   BIBLIOGRAPHIES

Albion, Robert Greenhalgh. Naval and Maritime History, An Annotated
    Bibliography. 4th ed. Mystic, Connecticut: Munson Institute of
    American Maritime History, The Marine Historical Association,
    1972.

Ballert, Albert G., comp. Bibliography, Great Lakes Research Checklist.
    Ann Arbor, Michigan: Great Lakes Commission, (c. 1962) - present,
    39 issues. (Published periodically.)

Bibliography, Great Lakes, Operation and Management of Freight Boats,
    Development of Commerce, Life and Training of Seamen. October
    19, 1914. (Available at the Great Lakes Historical Society,
    Vermilion, Ohio.)

Cleveland Public Library, comp. Bibliography, The Great Lakes and
     Related Subjects: Magazine Articles in the Cleveland Public
     Library. Cleveland: Cleveland Public Library, 1930.

_____. Bibliography, The Great Lakes: Early Travels. Cleveland:
     Cleveland Public Library, September 1931.

_____. The Great Lakes: Some Material in American Historical Society
     Publication. Cleveland: Cleveland Public Library, 1931.

General Services Administration. National Archives and Records Service.
     Reference Report: Information About Shipwrecks. Washington: n.d.

Greenwood, John O. Great Lakes Ships and Shipping - Current Sources of
     Information: A Bibliography of Source Materials. Chicago: 1958.
     (Available from the Great Lakes Historical Society, Vermilion,
     Ohio.)

Hanson, Agnes O., and Hauck, Helen. "Business and Technology Sources:
     Great Lakes Basin, Part I." Bulletin of the Business Information
     and Science and Technology Departments of the Cleveland Public
     Library 41 (April-June 1970).

_____."Business and Technology Sources: Great Lakes Basin, Part II."
     Bulletin of the Business Information and Science and Technology
     Departments of the Cleveland Public Library 41 (July-September
     1970.)

Jewell, Frank. Annotated Bibliography of Chicago History. Chicago:
     Chicago Historical Society, 1979.

Karpinski, Louis C. Bibliography of the Printed Maps of Michigan 1804-
     1880. Lansing, Michigan: Michigan Historical Commission, 1931;
     reprint ed., Amsterdam: Meridan Publishing Co., 1977. (Accompan-
     ied by an Atlas.)

McDermott, P. W. "Lake Erie Exploration to 1800: A Selected List of
     Source Materials in the Cleveland Public Library." Inland Seas
     1 (April 1945): 2-7.

Meyer, Herman H. B., comp. List of References on Shipping and Ship
     Building. Washington: Library of Congress, 1919.

Milwaukee Public Library: Local History and Marine Room. Books Dealing With Diving and Shipwrecks. Milwaukee: Milwaukee Public Library (c. 1980).

Minnesota Historical Society. Historic Resources in Minnesota. St. Paul: Minnesota Historical Society, 1978.

Noble, Dennis L., comp. United States Life-Saving Service Annotated Bibliography. Washington: U. S. Coast Guard Public Affairs Division, 1975.

Nobles, Richard, Challis, Steven, Collins, Laurie, Doxtator, Deborah, and Watson, Flo. "Bibliography of Great Lakes Marine History." (Unpublished Manuscript.) Kingston, Ontario: Marine Museum of the Great Lakes at Kingston, 1979.

Russel, Ruth Ida. One Hundred Years of Travel and Trade on the Great Lakes, 1800-1900: A Selected Bibliography. Madison, Wisconsin: Library School of the University of Wisconsin, 1939.

Schultz, Charles Roy. Bibliography of Maritime and Naval History: Periodical Articles During 1970. Mystic, Connecticut: The Marine Historical Association, 1971.

Strobridge, Truman, comp. United States Coast Guard Annotated Bibliography. Washington: U. S. Coast Guard Public Affairs Division, 1975.

Towle, Edward L. Bibliography on the Economic History and Geography of the Great Lakes - St. Lawrence Basin. Rochester, New York: University of Rochester, 1964.

_____. Bibliography on the Economic History and Geography of the Great Lakes - St. Lawrence Drainage Basin, Supplementary List No. 1. Rochester, New York: University of Rochester, 1964.

U. S. Department of Commerce, Maritime Administration, Great Lakes Region. Bibliography: Great Lakes Domestic Shipping History Course and Great Lakes Domestic Business Course. Cleveland: August 1980.

1-C.   DICTIONAIRES AND ENCYCLOPEDIAS OF NAUTICAL TERMINOLOGY AND HISTORY

Falconer, William. An Universal Dictionary of the Marine. London: T. Cadell, 1784.

Kemp, Peter, ed. The Oxford Companion to Ships and The Sea. London: Oxford University Press, 1976.

McEwen, W. A., and Lewis, A. H. Encyclopedia of Nautical Knowledge. Cambridge, Maryland: Cornell Maritime Press, 1953.

Tryckare, T. The Lore of Ships. Gothenburg, Sweden: A. B. Nordbook, 1975.

The Visual Encyclopedia of Nautical Terms. New York: Crown Publishers, 1978.

1-D.   FINDING GUIDES FOR BOOKS, MANUSCRIPTS, NEWSPAPERS, ETC.

American Library Association. The National Union Catalog, Pre-1956 Imprints. Chicago: American Library Association, v. 1-754, 1968-81.

Gutgesell, Stephen. Guide to Ohio Newspapers. Columbus: Ohio Historical Society, 1974.

Hammer, Philip, ed. A Guide to Archives and Manuscripts in the United States. New Haven, Conneticut: Yale Univeristy Press, 1961.

Johnson, Pam. Educators' Guide to Great Lakes Materials. University of Wisconsin Sea Grant College Program, Publication #600. Madison: University of Wisconsin, May 1978.

Library of Congress Catalogs. The National Union Catalog, Post-1956 Imprints. Published at various times by J. W. Edwards, Rowmann & Littlefield and currently Library of Congress, 1948 to present.

Library of Congress Catalogs. Newspapers in Microform, United States, 1948-1972 and 1973-1977. Washington: 1973 and 1978.

Marra, Jean M., ed. Readers' Guide to Periodical Literature. New York: H. W. Wilson Co., 1900 to present.

Michigan Newspapers on Microfilm. 5th ed. Lansing, Michigan: Michigan
      State Board of Education, State Library, 1980.

Milner, Anita Cheek. Newspaper Indexes: A Location and Subject Guide
      for Researchers. 3 vols. Metuchen, New Jersey: Scarecrow Press,
      1977-82.

Newspapers Available at Chicago Historical Society. Chicago: Chicago
      Historical Society, 1981.

Schultz, Charles R., comp. Inventory of the T. A. Scott Company, Inc.
      Papers 1889-1927. Mystic, Conneticut: Mystic Seaport Library,
      The Marine Historical Association, 1964.

Scott, Franklin William. Newspapers and Periodicals of Illinois, 1814-
      1879. Springfield, Illinois, 1910.

U. S. National Archives, Washington, D.C.
          .Catalog of National Archives Microfilm Publications (No. M248),
          1974.
          .Guide to the National Archives of the United States, 1974.
          .Guide to Cartographic Records in the National Archives, 1971.
          .Guide to the Records in the National Archives, 1975.
          .Inventory of Federal Archives in the States.
          .Miscellaneous Material National Archives.
          .National Archives of the United States, 1936.
          .Prologue; the Journal of the National Archives (Published three
          times yearly).
          .Select List of Publications of the National Archives and Records
          Service, 1977.

U. S. National Historical Publications and Records Commission, National
      Archives and Record Service. Directory of Archives and Manu-
      script Repositories. Washington: General Services Administration,
      1978.

2 - GREAT LAKES HISTORY

2-A.   GENERAL GREAT LAKES HISTORY

Agassiz, Louis. Lake Superior. Boston: Gould, Kendall & Lincoln, 1850.

Anderson, Melville B., trans. Relation of the Discoveries and Voyages
    of Cavelier de LaSalle from 1679 to 1681: The Official Narrative.
    Chicago: Caxton Club, 1901.

Ault, Phil. These Are The Great Lakes. New York: Dodd, Mead & Co., 1972.

Barcus, Frank. Freshwater Fury. Detroit: Wayne State University Press,
    1960.

Bowen, Dana Thomas. Lore of the Lakes. Cleveland: Freshwater Press, 1940.

_____. Memories of the Lakes. Cleveland: Freshwater Press, 1940.

Boyer, Dwight. Great Stories of the Great Lakes. New York: Dodd, Mead &
    Co., 1966.

_____. True Tales of the Great Lakes. New York: Dodd, Mead & Co., 1971.

_____. Strange Adventures of the Great Lakes. New York: Dodd, Mead &
    Co., 1974.

_____. Ships and Men of the Great Lakes. New York: Dodd, Mead & Co.,
    1977.

Campbell, Henry C. Early Days on the Great Lakes. Toronto: McClelland &
    Stewart, 1971.

Caruso, John Anthony. The Great Lakes Frontier. New York: Bobbs-Merrill
    Co., 1961.

Channing, Edward, and Lansing, Marion Florence. The Story of the Great
    Lakes. New York: Macmillan Co., 1909.

Curwood, James Oliver. The Great Lakes: The Vessels That Plough Them: Their Owners, Their Sailors, and Their Cargoes, Together With a Brief History of Our Inland Seas. New York: G. P. Putnam's Sons, 1909.

Cuthbertson, George A. Freshwater, a History and Narrative of the Great Lakes. New York: Macmillan Co., 1931.

Ellis, William Donohue. Land of the Inland Seas: The Historic and Beautiful Great Lakes Country. Palo Alto, California: American West, 1974.

Garriott, Edward B. Storms of the Great Lakes. Washington: Weather Bureau, 1903.

Hatcher, Harlan. The Great Lakes. New York: Oxford University Press, 1944.

_____. Lake Erie. New York: Bobbs-Merrill Co., 1945.

_____. The Western Reserve. Indianapolis: Bobbs-Merrill Co., 1949.

Hatcher, Harlan, and Walter, Erich A. A Pictorial History of the Great Lakes. New York: Crown Publishers, 1963.

Havighurst, Walter. The Long Ships Passing. New York: Macmillan Co., 1944.

_____. The Great Lakes Reader. New York: Macmillan Co., 1966.

Hennepin, Father Louis. A New Discovery of a Vast Country in America. 2 vols. London: M. Bentley, J. Tonson, H. Bontwick, T. Goodwin & S. Manship, 1698; reprint ed. by Reuben Gold Thwaites, ed., Chicago: A. C. McClurg & Co., 1903.

Lanman, James H. History of Michigan, Civil and Topographical, In a Compendious Form; With a View of the Surrounding Lakes. New York: E. French, 1839.

Landon, Fred. Lake Huron. New York: Bobbs-Merrill Co., 1944.

McKee, Russell. Great Lakes County. New York: Crowell, 1966.

Mansfield, J. B., ed. History of the Great Lakes. v. 1. Chicago: J. H. Beers & Co., 1899; reprint ed., Cleveland: Freshwater Press, 1972.

Mills, James Cooke. Our Inland Seas: Their Shipping and Commerce For Three Centuries. Chicago: A. C. McClurg & Co., 1919; reprint ed., Cleveland: Freshwater Press, 1976.

Nute, Grace Lee. Lake Superior. New York: Bobbs-Merrill Co., 1944.

Olson, David C. Life on the Upper Michigan Frontier. Boston: Branden Press, 1974.

Parkman, Francis. The Discovery of the Great West: LaSalle. New York: Rinehart & Co., 1956.

Plumb, Ralph G. History of Navigation of the Great Lakes, 61st Congress, 3rd Session, House Committee on Railways and Canals. Washington: 1887.

_____. Lake Michigan. Manitowoc, Wisconsin: Brandt Printing & Binding Co., 1941.

Pound, Arthur. Lake Ontario. New York: Bobbs-Merrill Co., 1945.

Quaife, Milo M. Lake Michigan. New York: Bobbs-Merrill Co., 1945.

University of Wisconsin Sea Grant Program. Our Great Lakes. Madison, University of Wisconsin, September 1973.

Snider, C. J. H. "Schooner Days." A Numbered Weekly Series of Articles in the Toronto Evening Telegram January 30, 1931 to January 5, 1959.

Thwaites, Reuben Gold, ed. The Jesuit Relations and Allied Documents: Travels and Explorations of the Jesuit Missionaries in New France 1610-1791. 73 vols. Cleveland: Burrows Brothers Co., 1896-1901.

Whitlark, Frederick Louis. Introduction to the Lakes. New York: Greenwich Book Publishers, 1959.

Winsor, Justin. Cartier to Frontenac. New York: Franklin, 1894.

Wood, William C. H. All Afloat: A Chronicle of Craft and Waterways. Toronto: University of Toronto Press, 1964.

Anderson, Charles. Isle of View: A History of South Manitou Island. Frankfort, Michigan: J. B. Publications, 1979.

Andreas, Alfred Theodore. History of Chicago. 3 vols. Chicago: By the Author, 1884-86.

Barry, James P. Georgian Bay: The Sixth Great Lake. Toronto: Clarke, Irwin & Co., 1978.

Bayliss, Joseph E. and Estelle L., and Quaife, Milo M. River of Destiny: The Saint Marys. Detroit: Wayne State University, 1955.

Beaver Island Historical Society. The Journal of Beaver Island History. 2 vols. St. James, Michigan: Beaver Island Historical Society, 1980.

Burnham, Guy M. The Lake Superior Country in History and Story. Ann Arbor, Michigan: Browzer Books, 1974.

Burton, Clarence Monroe. The City of Detroit, Michigan, 1701-1922. 5 vols. Detroit: S. J. Clarke Publishing Co., 1922.

_____. History of Wayne County. 4 vols. Detroit: S. J. Clarke Publishing Co., 1930.

Coffman, Edna M. Mackinaw City Settlers and The Savage Straits. Grand Marais, Michigan: Voyager Press, 1976.

Cronyn, Margaret, and Kenny, John. The Saga of Beaver Island. Ann Arbor, Michigan: Braun & Brumfield, 1958.

Deluca, Helen R. The Lake Erie Isles and How They Got Their Names. Bellevue, Ohio: The Historic Lyme Church Association, 1974.

Ellis, William Donohue. The Cuyahoga. Dayton, Ohio: Landfall Press, 1976.

Farmer, Silas. History of Detroit and Wayne County. Detroit: Silas Farmer and Co., 1884.

Havighurst, Walter. Three Flags at the Straits: The Forts of Mackinac. Englewood Cliffs, New Jersey: Prentiss-Hall, 1966.

Ingalls, Hon. E. S. Centennial History of Menominee County. Menominee, Michigan: n.p., 1876.

Jenks, William Lee. History of St. Clair County. 2 vols. Chicago: Lewis Publishing Co., 1912.

Jewell, Frank. Annotated Bibliography of Chicago History. Chicago: Chicago Historical Society, 1979.

LaFayette, Kenneth D. Flaming Brands: Fifty Years of Iron Making in the Upper Peninsula of Michigan, 1848-1898. Marquette, Michigan: Northern Michigan University Press, 1977.

Lauristan, Victor. Romantic Kent. Chatham, Ontario: Corporation of the County of Kent, 1952.

McElroy, Frank. A Short History of Marine City, Michigan. Marine City, Michigan: Marine City Rotary Club, 1980.

Metcalfe, Willis. Marine Memories. Picton, Ontario: Picton Gazette Publishing Co., 1976,

Moore, Charles. History of Michigan. 3 vols. Chicago: Lewis Publishing Co., 1915.

Morrison, Neil. Garden Gateway to Canada. Toronto: Ryerson Press, 1954.

Newton, Stanley. The Story of Sault Ste. Marie and Chippewa County. Sault Ste. Marie, Michigan: Sault News Printing Co., 1923.

Ranville, Judy, and Campbell, Nancy. Memories of Mackinaw. Mackinaw City, Michigan: Mackinaw City Public Library, 1976.

Ratigan, William. Straits of Mackinac: Crossroads of the Great Lakes. Grand Rapids, Michigan: Wm. B. Eerdmans Publishing Co., 1957.

Ryan, James A. The Town of Milan. Sandusky, Ohio: By the Author, 1928.

Smith, Thomas A. Oulanie Thepy: The Golden Age of Harbour Town
     Vermilion 1837 to 1879. Bowling Green, Ohio: Northwest Ohio-
     Great Lakes Research Center, 1973.

Shurtleff, Mary Belle. Old Arbre Croche: A Factual and Comprehensive
     History of Cross Village, Michigan. Cross Village, Michigan:
     By the Author, 1963; reprint ed., Richard A. Pohrt, 1975.

Strickland, William Peter. Old Mackinac or, The Fortress of the Lakes
     and Its Surroundings. Philadelphia: James Challen & Son, 1860.

Vent, Myron H. South Manitou Island: From Pioneer Community to National
     Park. Springfield, Virginia: Goodway Press, 1973.

White, James. "Place-Names in Georgian Bay Including the North Channel."
     Papers and Records of the Ontario Historical Society 11 (1913): 5.

White, Wallace B. "The Ghost Port of Milan and A Druid Moon." Inland Seas
     6 and 7 (1950 and 1951).

Williams, Ralph D. The Honorable Peter White: A Biographical Sketch of
     the Lake Superior Iron Country. Cleveland: Penton Publishing Co.,
     1905.

Wood, Edwin O. Historic Mackinac. 2 vols. New York: Macmillan Co., 1918.

2-C.   GREAT LAKES MARITIME HISTORY

1.   Commerce and Trade

Andress, Frank. Grain Movements in the Great Lakes Region. U. S. Depart-
     ment of Agriculture, Bureau of Statistics, Bulletin No. 81.
     Washington, 1910.

Barton, James L. Commerce of the Lakes, and Erie Canal. Buffalo: Beaver's
     Power Presses, 1851.

Beasley, Norman. Freighters of Fortune: The Story of the Great Lakes. New York: Harper & Brothers Publishers, 1930.

Brownwell, G. "The Role of the Lake Package Freighters, Southwest Ontario." M.A. thesis, Western Ontario University, 1951.

Carse, Robert. The Great Lakes Story. New York: Norton, 1968.

Draine, E. H."Import Traffic of Chicago and Its Hinterland." Ph.D. thesis, University of Chicago, 1963.

Hartshorne, Richard. "The Lake Traffic of Chicago." Ph.D. thesis, University of Chicago, 1924.

Innis, Harold A. The Fur Trade in Canada. Toronto: University of Toronto Press, 1930.

MacGibbon, D. A. The Canadian Grain Trade. Toronto: Macmillan Co., 1932.

Mason, Philip. The History of Great Lakes Transportation. Ann Arbor, Michigan: Brown-Branfield, 1957.

McPhedran, Marie. Cargoes on the Great Lakes. Toronto: Macmillan Company of Canada, 1952.

Odle, Thomas D. "The American Grain Trade of the Great Lakes, 1825-1873." Ph.D. thesis, University of Michigan, 1952. (Listed in Dissertation Abstracts 12 (1952): 180, Film 1059. Also appeared serially in Inland Seas 1951 to 1953.)

Reiter, George. Log Transportation in the Great Lakes States, 1840-1918. Glendale, California: Arthur H. Clark Co., 1953.

Ritter, Alfred H. Transportation Economics of the Great Lakes - St. Lawrence Ship Channel. Washington: Great Lakes-St. Lawrence Tidewater Association, 1925.

Tunell, George Gerard. Transportation on the Great Lakes of North America. A dissertation submitted at the University of Chicago. Also House Document No. 277, 55th Congress, 2nd Session, 1898.

U. S. Board of Engineers for Rivers and Harbors, and U. S. Shipping
    Board. Transportation on the Great Lakes. Washington: 1926 ff.

U. S. Engineer Department."Commerce of the Lakes and Western Rivers."
    30th Congress, 1st Session. Executive Document No. 19. House of
    Representatives. Letter from the Secretary of War, 1848.

U. S. Treasury Department. Report on the Trade and Commerce of the
    British North American Colonies, and Upon the Trade of the Great
    Lakes and Rivers, by Israel D. Andrews. Washington: Beverley
    Tucker, Senate Printer, 1854.

U. S. Secretary of the Treasury. Statistics of Lake Commerce, by George
    G. Tunell. A Report Made to the Bureau of Statistics.
    Washington: Government Printing Office, 1898.

Workman, James C. "Shipping on the Great Lakes." Historical Transactions
    1893-1943. New York: The Society of Naval Architects and Marine
    Engineers, 1945.

2.   Captains and Crews

Gjerset, Knut. Norwegian Sailors on the Great Lakes. Northfield, Minn-
    esota: Norwegian-American Historical Association, 1928; reprint
    ed., New York: Arno Press, 1979.

Great Lakes Red Book. St. Clair Shores, Michigan: Fourth Seacost Pub-
    lishing Co. Current annual since 1902. Originally published by
    Penton Publishing Co., Cleveland. (Contains a list of captains
    and marine engineers.)

Mansfield, J. B., ed. History of the Great Lakes. v. 2. Chicago: J. H.
    Beers & Co., 1899; reprint ed., Cleveland: Freshwater Press, 1972.

R. L. Polk and Company's Marine Directory of the Great Lakes. Detroit: R.
    L. Polk & Co., 1884, 1888, 1891. (Contains a list of vessel cap-
    tians and their city of residence.)

Richter, Charles. Mariners' Manual of the Great Lakes. Cleveland: n.p.,
    1938.

Ship Masters' Association of the Great Lakes. Annual Directory of Names,
     Pennant Numbers and Addresses of All Members. Cleveland: Marine
     Review Print and various other printers or publishers for differ-
     ent editions. Name later changed to International Shipmasters'
     Association. 1893 to 1967.

⚓

3.   Commercial, Technical and Fraternal Organizations (and Their Concern

American Bureau of Shipping. One Hundredth Anniversary, 1862-1962. New
     York: American Bureau of Shipping, 1962.

Directory and Manual of the Licensed Tugmen's Protective Association of
     America. Great Lakes Edition,(1908-?).

Great Lakes Protective Association. Annual Report. Cleveland: Great Lakes
     Protective Association.

Hoagland, Henry E. Wage Bargaining on the Vessels of the Great Lakes.
     Urbana: University of Illinois, 1917.

Lake Carriers' Association. Annual Report of the Lake Carriers' Assoc-
     iation. Detroit: Winn & Hammond, 1907 to present. (At various
     times published in different locations by different publishers.)

_____. The Bulletin. Cleveland: Lake Carriers' Association, 1911 to
     present. (Printed periodically during the shipping season.)

Luckenbach, Lewis. "American Bureau of Shipping 1862-1943." Historical
     Transactions 1893-1943. New York: Society of Naval Architects and
     Marine Engineers, 1945.

Robert, William P. "Formation of the Society of Naval Architects and
     Marine Engineers." Historical Transactions 1893-1943. New York:
     Society of Naval Architects and Marine Engineers, 1945.

Ship Masters' Association of the Great Lakes: A Directory. (See Section
     2-C-2.)

Society of Naval Architects and Marine Engineers. Index to Transactions,
     1893-1943. New York: Society of Naval Architects & Marine Engin-
     eers, 1946.

Barry, James P. The Battle of Lake Erie, September 10, 1813: The Naval Battle That Decided a Northern U. S. Boundary. New York: Franklin Watts, 1970.

Bunnell, David C. The Travels and Adventures of David C. Bunnell During 23 Years of Seafaring Life. Palmyra, New York: J. H. Borles, 1831. (Personal account of one of the crewmembers on Perry's flagship the LAWRENCE.)

Dillon, Richard. We have Met The Enemy - Oliver Hazard Perry: Wilderness Commodore. New York: McGraw-Hill Book Co., 1978.

Dobbins, W. W. The Battle of Lake Erie and Reminiscences of the Flagships "LAWRENCE" and "NIAGARA." 3rd ed. Erie, Pennsylvania: Ashby Printing Co., 1929.

Hitsman, J. Mackay. The Incredible War of 1812. Toronto: University of Toronto Press, 1965.

MacKenzie, Alexander S. The Life of Commodore Oliver Hazard Perry. 2 vols. New York: A. L. Fowle, 1900.

Mills, James Cooke. Oliver Hazard Perry and the Battle of Lake Erie. Detroit: John Phelps, 1913.

Musham, Harry Albert. "Early Great Lakes Steamboats: The Battle of the Windmill and Afterward, 1838-1842." The American Neptune 8 (1948): 1-24.

_____. "Early Great Lakes Steamboats: Warships and Iron Hulls, 1841-1846." The American Neptune 8 (1948); 1-18.

"Perry's Account of the Battle of Lake Erie, 1813." Old South Leaflets No. 204 9 (August 1909): 201-222. Boston: Directors of the Old South Work, 1909.

Reibel, Daniel B. "The British Navy on the Upper Great Lakes 1760-1789." Niagra Frontier (1973).

Roosevelt, Theodore. The Naval War of 1812. New York: G. P. Putnam's Sons, 1882. (Four editions, 1882-1902.)

Rosenberg, Max. The Building of Perry's Fleet on Lake Erie, 1812-1813. Harrisburg, Pennsylvania: Pennsylvania Historical and Museum Commission, 1950.

Snider, C. H. J. Tarry Breeks and Velvet Garters: Sail on the Great Lakes of America. Toronto: Ryerson Press, 1958.

Spencer, Herbert R. USS MICHIGAN, USS WOLVERINE. Erie, Pennsylvania: Erie Book Store, 1966.

U. S. Congress, House Committee on Naval Affairs. The Naval Defense of the Great Lakes. 37th Congress, 3rd Session, Report No. 4. Washington: 1863.

5.   *Canals*

Aitken, Hugh G. J. The Welland Canal Company: A Study in Canadian Enterprise. Cambridge: Harvard University Press, 1954.

Andrist, Ralph K. The Erie Canal. New York: American Heritage Publishing Co., 1964.

Beck, M. C. "An Historical Evaluation of the St. Lawrence Seaway Controversy, 1950-1953." Ph.D. thesis, St. John's University, 1954.

Clowes, Ernest S. Shipways to the Sea: Our Inland Coastal Waterways. Baltimore: Williams & Wilkins Co., 1929.

Coombs, Albert E. History of the Niagara Peninsula and the New Welland Canal. Toronto: Historical Publishers Association, 1939.

Dickinson, J. N. "The Canal at Sault Ste. Marie, Michigan: Inception, Construction, Operation, and the Canal Grant Lands." Ph.D. thesis, University of Wisconsin, 1967.

Drago, Harry Sinclair. Canal Days in America. New York: Bramkall House, 1972.

Fleming, George J., Sr. "Canal at Chicago: A Study in Political and Social History." Ph.D. thesis, University of America, 1951.

Fowle, Otto. Sault Ste. Marie and Its Great Waterways. New York: G. P. Putnam's Sons, 1925.

Franchere, Ruth. Westward by Canal: The Story of the Great Canal Era. New York: Macmillan, 1972.

Geddes, George. "The Erie Canal." Publications of the Buffalo Historical Society 2 (1879): 263-304.

Hadfield, Charles. The Canal Age. New York: Frederick A. Praeger, 1968.

Hawley, Merwin S. "The Erie Canal: Its Origin, Its Success and Its Necessity." Read before the Buffalo Historical Club, February 3, 1863.

Ireland, Tom. The Great Lakes - St. Lawrence Deep Waterway to the Sea. New York: G. P. Putnam's Sons, 1934.

Jackson, John N. Welland and the Welland Canal. Belleville, Ontario: Welland Canal By-Pass, Mika Publishing Co., 1975.

Judson, Clara Ingram. The Mighty Soo. Chicago: Follett Publishing Co., 1976.

Kingsford, Wm. The Canadian Canals: Their History and Cost. Toronto: Rollo & Adam, 1865.

McDougall, John L. "The Welland Canal to 1841." M. A. thesis, University of Toronto, 1923.

Mabee, Carleton. The Seaway Story. New York: Macmillan & Co., 1961.

MacElwee, Roy S., and Ritter, Alfred H. Economic Aspects of the Great Lakes-St. Lawrence Ship Channel. New York: Ronald Press Co., 1921.

Melvin, David Skene. The Welland Canals: Historical Resource Analysis and Preservation Alternatives. Toronto: Ontario Ministry of Culture & Recreation, 1979.

Moore, Charles, ed. The St. Mary's Falls Canal Semi-Centennial, 1905. Detroit: Semi-Centennial Commission, 1907.

Ryan, James A. The Town of Milan. Sandusky, Ohio: By the Author, 1928.

Shaw, R. E."A History of the Erie Canal, 1807-1850, With Particular
    Reference to Western New York." Ph.D. thesis, University of
    Rochester, 1954.

⚓

6.   Harbors and Ports

Baxter, Henry H., and Heyl, Erik. Maps, Buffalo Harbor, 1804-1964.
    Buffalo: Buffalo & Erie County Historical Society, 1965.

Beckett, William C. A Brief History of the Port of Toledo. Toledo:
    Toledo-Lucas County Port Authority, 1961.

Butterfield, George E. Bay County Past and Present. Bay City, Michigan:
    Bay City Board of Education, 1918.

Carter, James L. Voyageur's Harbor, Grand Marais. Grand Marais,
    Michigan: Pilot Press, 1967.

Derby, W. E."A History of the Port of Milwaukee, 1835-1910." Ph.D.
    thesis, University of Wisconsin, 1963.

Finn, J. Leo. Old Shipping Days in Oswego. Oswego, New York: Oswego
    County Board of Supervisors, 1976.

Hall, Steve. Duluth-Superior Harbor Cultural Resources Study. St. Paul:
    U. S. Army Corps of Engineers, 1976.

Hamming, Edward. The Port of Milwaukee. Rock Island, Illinois: Augustana
    Library Publications, 1953.

Kitchel, Mary D. Spring Lake Community Centennial. Spring Lake, Michigan:
    By the Author, 1969.

LesStrang, Jacques. The Great Lakes Ports of North America. Ann Arbor,
    Michigan: LesStrang Publishing Co., 1973.

Lillie, Leo C. Historic Grand Haven and Ottawa County. Grand Haven,
        Michigan: By the Author, 1931.

Marine History of the Lakes Ports. Detroit: Detroit Historical
        Publishing Co., 1877.

Rapp, M. A. "The Port of Buffalo, 1825-1880." Ph.D. thesis, Duke
        University, 1948.

Sargent, John H. The Development of Cleveland's Harbor. Cleveland:
        Western Reserve Historical Society, 1892.

Schenker, Eric. The Port of Milwaukee: An Economic Review. Madison,
        Wisconsin: The University of Wisconsin Press, 1967.

Symons, Thomas."History of Buffalo Harbor." Publications of the Buffalo
        Historical Society 5 (1902): 239.

Wood, George Emery."Commercial Aspects of the Port of Milwaukee." M.A.
        thesis, University of Wisconsin, 1923.

Zercher, F. K."An Economic History of the Port of Oswego." Ph.D. thesis,
        Syracuse University, 1935.

2-D. GREAT LAKES GEOGRAPHY AND TRAVEL ACCOUNTS

Anderson, Melville B., trans. Relation of the Discoveries and Voyages
        of Cavelier de LaSalle from 1679 to 1681: The Official Narrative.
        Chicago: Caxton Club, 1901.

Cantor, George. Great Lakes Guidebook, Lake Huron and Eastern Lake
        Michigan. Ann Arbor, Michigan: University of Michigan Press, 1978.

_____. Great Lakes Guidebook, Lakes Ontario and Erie. Ann Arbor,
        Michigan: Unversity of Michigan Press, 1978.

_____. Great Lakes Guidebook, Lake Superior and Western Lake Michigan.
        Ann Arbor, Michigan: Universtiy of Michigan Press, 1980.

Carver, Jonathon. Travels Through the Interior Part of North America in
        the Years 1766, 1767 and 1768. 3rd ed. London: C. Dilly, 1781.

Cox, E. G. A Reference Guide to the Literature of Travel Including
    Voyages, Geographical Descriptions, Adventures, Shipwrecks and
    Expeditions. Seattle, Washington: University of Seattle, 1935.

Cumming, W. P., et al. The Exploration of North America 1630-1776.
    New York: G. P. Putnam's Sons, 1974.

Disturnell, John. A Trip Through the Lakes of North America. New York:
    By the Author, 1857.

_____. The Great Lakes, or Inland Seas of America. New York: Charles
    Scribner, 1863.

_____. Sailing on the Great Lakes and Rivers of America. Philadelphia:
    By the Author, 1874.

Gilman, Chandler R. Life on the Lakes Being Tales and Sketches Collected
    During a Trip to the Pictured Rocks of Lake Superior. 2 vols. New
    York: George Dearborn Co., 1836.

St. John, John. A True Description of the Lake Superior Country. New York:
    Wm. H. Graham, 1846; reprint ed., Grand Rapids, Michigan: Black
    Letter Press, 1976.

Schoolcraft, Henry R. Narrative Journals of Travels From Detroit North-
    west Through the Great Chain of American Lakes to the Sources of
    the Mississippi River in the Year 1820. Albany, New York: E. & E.
    Hosford, 1821; reprint ed., n.p.: Arno Press, Inc., 1970.

_____. Summary Narrative of an Exploratory Expedition to the Sources
    of the Mississippi River in 1820: Resumed and Completed, by the
    Discovery of Its Origin in Itasca Lake, in 1832. Philadelphia:
    Lippincott, Grambo & Co., 1855; reprint ed., New York: Kraus
    Reprint Co., 1973.

Waldron, Webb, and Waldron, Marion Patton. We Explore the Great Lakes.
    New York: Century Co., 1923.

Whitcomb, D. C. A Lake Tour to Picturesque Mackinac. Detroit: Detroit &
    Cleveland Steam Navigation Co., 1884.

3-A.   GENERAL SHIP HISTORY

Anderson, Romola, and R. C. The Sailing Ship: Six Thousand Years of
     History. London: G. G. Harrap & Co., 1926.

Buchanan, Lamont. Ships of Steam. New York: McGraw-Hill Book Co., 1956.

Chappelle, Howard I. The History of American Sailing Ships. New York:
     W. W. Norton & Co., 1935. (Through 1973, Chapelle has written
     at least seven other books which taken together represent the
     best complete history of American sailing vessels. Also, the
     series of books by W. A. Baker are excellent. Reference to these
     and like volumes can be found in the Albion bibliography.)

Chatterton, E. Keble. Sailing Ships: The Story of Their Development from
     the Earliest Times to the Present Day. London: Sidgwick & Jackson,
     1909.

_____. Fore and Aft: The Story of the Fore and Aft Rig from the
     Earliest Times to the Present Day. Philadelphia: J. B. Lippincott
     Co., 1912.

Croil, James. Steam Navigation and Its Relation to the Commerce of Canada
     and the United States. Toronto: Wm. Briggs, 1898.

Culver, Henry B., and Grant, Gordon. The Book of Old Ships. New York:
     Garden City Publication Co., 1924.

Dornfeld, A. A. "Chicago's Age of Sail." Chicago Historical Society, New
     Series 2 (1973): 156-165.

Hunnewell, Frederick A. "Revenue Cutters, Coast Guard Ships and Light-
     ships." Historical Transactions 1893-1943. New York: Society of
     Naval Architects & Marine Engineers, 1945.

Laing, Alexander. American Sail: A Pictorial History. New York: E. P.
     Dutton & Co., 1961.

_____. The American Heritage History of Seafaring America. New York:
     American Heritage Publishing Co., 1974.

Morris, E. P. The Fore-and-Aft Rig in America: A Sketch. New Haven,
    Connetticut: Yale University Press, 1927.

Morrison, John H. History of American Steam Navigation. New York: Stephen
    Daye Press, 1958.

Rogers, Stanley R. H. The Book of the Sailing Ship. New York: Thomas Y.
    Crowell Co., 1931.

Wallace, Frederick William. Wooden Ships and Iron Men. Belleville,
    Ontario: Mika Studio, 1973.

3-B.   GREAT LAKES SHIP HISTORY

Anderson, Melville B., trans. Relation of the Discoveries and Voyages of
    Cavelier de LaSalle from 1679 to 1681: The Official Narrative.
    Chicago: Caxton Club, 1901. (Contains an official account by
    Hennepin of the building and first voyage of the GRIFFON.)

Barkhausen, Henry N. The Ships and Sailing Albums, Book 2: Great Lakes
    Sailing Ships. Milwaukee: Kalmbach Publishing Co., 1947.

Barry, James P. Ships of the Great Lakes: 300 Years of Navigation. 2nd
    ed. Berkeley, California: Howell-North Books, 1973.

Brownwell, G."The Role of the Lake Package Freighters, Southwest Ontario.
    Ph.D. thesis, Western Ontario University, 1951.

Buehr, Walter. Ships of the Great Lakes. New York: G. P. Putnam's Sons,
    1956.

Bugbee, Gordon P. The Lake Erie Sidewheel Steamers of Frank E. Kirby.
    Detroit: Great Lakes Model Shipbuilder's Guild, 1955.

Cumberland, B. "Canoe, Sail, and Steam: Early Navigation on the Great
    Lakes." Canadian Magazine 42 (November 1913): 85-92.

Curwood, James Oliver. The Great Lakes: The Vessels That Plough Them: Their Owners, Their Sailors, and Their Cargoes, Together with a Brief History of Our Inland Seas. New York: G. P. Putnam's Sons, 1909.

Cuthbertson, George A. Freshwater: A History and a Narrative of the Great Lakes. New York: Macmillan Co., 1931. (See Appendices for history and listing of early Great Lakes vessels.)

Dornfeld, A. A. "Steamships: A Hundred Years Ago." Chicago Historical Society, New Series 4 (1957): 148-156.

_____. "Steamships After 1871." Chicago Historical Society, New Series 6 (1977): 12-22.

Dowling, Rev. Edward J. The "Lakers" of World War I. Detroit: University of Detroit Press, 1967.

Ericson, Bernard E. "The Evolution of Great Lakes Ships: Part I - Sail." Inland Seas 25 (1969): 199-212.

_____. "The Evolution of Great Lakes Ships: Part II - Steam and Steel." Society of Naval Architects & Marine Engineers, 1968.

Fletcher, D. G. "A Study of Package Freight Carriers on the Great Lakes," Ph.D. thesis, University of Michigan, 1960. Dissertation Abstracts 21 (1960): 2137.

Hilton, George W. The Great Lakes Car Ferries. Berkeley, California: Howell-North, 1962.

Hodge, William. The Pioneer Steamboats on Lake Erie. Buffalo: Printing House of Bigelow Brothers, 1883.

Howland, Henry R. "Navy Island and the First Successors to the GRIFFON." Publications of the Buffalo Historical Society 6 (1903): 17-33.

Lindblad, A. F. "A Critical Analysis of the Factors Affecting Safety and Operation of the Bulk Freight Vessels of the Great Lakes." Ph.D. thesis, University of Michigan, 1924.

Lydecker, Ryck. Pigboat - The Story of the Whalebacks. 2nd ed. Superior, Wisconsin: Head of the Lakes Maritime Society, 1981.

McCarthy, John Myron. "Economic Aspects in the Evolution of the Great Lakes Freighter." Ph.D. thesis, University of Southern California, 1971.

Metcalfe, Willis. Canvas and Steam on Quinte Waters. Picton, Ontario: Prince Edward Historical Society, 1965.

Michigan Department of Conservation. Great Lakes, Great Boats. Lansing, Michigan: Department of Conservation, n.d.

Mills, J. C. "Giant Ore Carriers on the Great Lakes." Cassier's Magazine 35 (November 1908): 109-119.

Musham, Harry Albert. "Early Great Lakes Steamboats, 1816-1830." The American Neptune 6 (1946): 1-18.

_____. "Early Great Lakes Steamboats: Westward Ho! And Flush Times 1831-1837." The American Neptune 7 (1947): 1-24.

_____. "Early Great Lakes Steamboats: The First Propellers, 1841-1845." The American Neptune 17 (1957): 89-104.

_____. "Early Great Lakes Steamboats: The Battle of the Windmill and Afterward, 1838-1842." The American Neptune 8 (1948): 1-24.

_____. "Early Great Lakes Steamboats: Warships and Iron Hulls, 1841-1846." The American Neptune 8 (1948): 1-18.

_____. "Early Great Lakes Steamboats: The Chicago Line, 1838-1839." The American Neptune 18 (1958): 273-300.

_____. "Early Great Lakes Steamboats: Hard Times and the ERIE Disaster, 1849-1841." The American Neptune 20 (1960): 79-103.

Wilterding, John A. McDougall's Dream. Sturgeon Bay, Wisconsin: Badger Bay Printers, 1979.

Burgtorf, Frances D. CHIEF WAWATAM. Cheboygan, Michigan: By the Author, 1976.

Burton, C. M. LaSalle and the GRIFFON. Historical Paper Delivered Before the Society of Colonial Wars of the State of Michigan, 1902. Detroit: Winn & Hammond, 1903.

Busch, Gregory James. Lake Huron's Death Ship. Saginaw, Michigan: Busch Oceanographic Equipment Co., 1975. (The PEWABIC.)

Clary, James. Ladies of the Lakes. Lansing, Michigan: Michigan Department of Natural Resources, 1981

Great Lakes Maritime Institute. Great Lakes Ships: Book No. 1, Photos of Captain Wm. J. Taylor. Detroit: Great Lakes Maritime Institute, 1965.

_____. Great Lakes Ships: Book No. 2, Photos by Pesha. Detroit: Great Lakes Maritime Institute, 1968.

Greenwood, John O. Namesakes of the Lakes. Cleveland: Freshwater Press, 1970.

_____. Namesakes II. Cleveland: Freshwater Press, 1973.

_____. Namesakes 1930-1955. Cleveland: Freshwater Press, 1978.

_____. Namesakes of the '80's. Cleveland: Freshwater Press, 1980.

_____. Namesakes 1956-1980. Cleveland: Freshwater Press, 1981.

Heyl, Erik. Early American Steamers. 6 vols. Buffalo: n.p., 1953-1969. (Includes a general index in v. 6.)

Jackman, J. Albin, and Bascom, John H., eds. Ahoy and Farewell. Detroit: Marine Historical Society of Detroit, 1970.

Lang, Steven, and Spectre, Peter H. On the Hawser, A Tugboat Album. Camden, Maine: Downeast Books, 1980.

LeLievre, Roger. The VALLEY CAMP Story: From an Ore Ship to a Museum Ship. Sault Ste. Marie, Michigan: Le Sault de Sainte Marie Historical Sites, 1975.

LesStrang, Jacques. Lake Carriers: The Saga of the Great Lakes Fleet. 1st ed. Seattle: Superior Publishing Co., 1977.

MacLean, Harrison John. The Fate of the GRIFFON. Chicago: Swallow Press, 1974.

Marine City Rotary Club. River District Bicentennial Photo Collection. Marine City, Michigan: Rotary Club, 1967.

Marine Historical Society of Detorit. Ships That Never Die. Detroit: Marine Historical Society of Detroit, 1952.

Marshall, O. H. The Building and Voyage of the GRIFFON in 1679. Buffalo: Bigelow Brothers, n.d.; reprint ed., Publications of the Buffalo Historical Society 1 (August 1870); 253-288.

Massman, Emory A. The Ship's Scene...Thru Massman's Lens. Detroit: Massman Photo Co., 1964.

Musham, Harry Albert. "Early Great Lakes Steamboats: The ONTARIO and the FRONTENAC." The American Neptune 3 (1943): 333-344.

_____. "Early Great Lakes Steamboats: The WALK-IN-THE-WATER." The American Neptune 5 (1945): 13-28.

_____. "Early Great Lakes Steamboats: The CAROLINE AFFAIR, 1837-1838." The American Neptune 7 (1947): 2-18.

Spencer, Herbert R. USS MICHIGAN, USS WOLVERINE. Erie, Pennsylvania: Erie Book Store, 1966.

Stanton, Samuel Ward. Great Lakes Steam Vessels. No. 1: American Steam Vessles Series. Meriden, Connecticut: Meriden Gravure Co., 1962.

Van der Linden, Rev. Peter J., ed., and the Marine Historical Society of Detroit. Great Lakes Ships We Remember. Cleveland: Freshwater Press, 1979.

Welnetz, Bob. Ships of the Great Lakes on Postcards. v. 1. Manitowoc,
     Wisconsin: Manitowoc Maritime Museum, 1976.

_____. Ships of the Great Lakes on Postcards. v. 2. Manitowoc,
     Wisconsin: Manitowoc Maritime Museum, 1977.

3-D.   SHIPS LISTINGS (Not Including Registers and Directories)

Cuthbertson, George A. Freshwater, A History and A Narrative of the Great
     Lakes. New York: Macmillan Co., 1931. (See Appendices for listing
     of early Great Lakes vessels.)

Lytle, William M., and Holdcamper, Forrest R., comp. Merchant Steam
     Vessels of the United States 1790-1868. "The Lytle-Holdcamper
     List." Staten Island, New York: Steamship Historical Society of
     America, 1952; revised and edited ed. by C. Bradford Mitchell and
     Kenneth R. Hall, 1975. (Includes Supplment No. 1, 1978.)

Mansfield, J. B. History of the Great Lakes. v. 1. Chicago: J. H. Beers
     & Co., 1899; reprint ed., Cleveland: Freshwater Press, 1972.
     (See Chapter 42, p. 787, for list of lake vessels.)

Mills, John M. Canadian Coastal and Inland Steam Vessels, 1809-1930.
     Providence, Rhode Island: Steamship Historical Society of America,
     1979.

_____. Supplement No. 1 to Canadian Coastal and Inland Steam Vessels,
     1809-1930. Providence, Rhode Island: Steamship Historical Society
     of America, 1981.

U. S. Department of Commerce Maritime Administration. United States and
     Canadian Great Lakes Fleets: Steam and Motor Ships of 1,000 Gross
     Tons and Over as of December 31, 1955. Washington: Maritime Admin-
     istration, Statistics & Special Studies Office, 1956 ff.

World Ship Society, Toronto Branch. Preliminary List of Canadian Merchant
     Steamships, 1809-1930. Toronto: World Ship Society, 1962.

Arnold Transit Company and Straits Transit, Inc. 100 Years of Passenger Travel. Booklet. Grand Marais, Michigan: Voyager Press, 1978.

Bugbee, Gordon P. "The North Shore Line - Part I and II." Telescope 21 (September/October 1972): 127-135 and (November/December 1972): 160-167.

Burton, Clarence M. The City of Detroit, Michigan, 1701-1922. v. 1. Detroit: S. J. Clarke Publishing Co., 1922. (See p. 679 for a brief history of shipping companies in the City of Detroit.)

Calvin, D. D. A Saga of the St. Lawrence. Toronto: Ryerson Press, 1954. (Calvin Company History.)

Dowling, Rev. Edward J. "The Winslow Fleet." Telescope 24 (May/June 1975): 68-81. (This citation is only exemplary of the numerous fleet lists and histories published by Father Dowling in serials such as Telescope and The Detroit Marine Historian.)

Duncan, F. "History of the Detroit and Cleveland Navigation Company, 1850-1951." Ph.D. thesis, University of Chicago, 1951. (Appeared serially in various editions of Inland Seas, 1951-1958.)

Elliott, James L. Red Stacks Over the Horizon: The Story of the Goodrich Steamboat Line. Grand Rapids, Michigan: William B. Eerdmans Publishing Co., 1967.

Frederickson, Arthur, and Lucy F. Pictorial History of the C & O Train and Auto Ferries and Pere Marquette Line Steamers. Revised ed. Ludington, Michigan: Lakeside Printing Co., 1965.

Hatcher, Harlan. A Century of Iron and Men. Indianapolis: Bobbs-Merrill, 1950. (Cleveland Cliffs History.)

Havighurst, Walter. Vein of Iron: The Pickands Mather Story. Cleveland: World Publishing Co., 1958.

Meakin, Alexander C. "Four Long and One Short: A History of the Great Lakes Towing Company." Published serially in Inland Seas from 1974 to 1978.

Musham, Harry Albert. "Early Great Lakes Steamboats: The Chicago Line, 1838-1839." The American Neptune 18 (1958): 273-300.

Ramsden, M. C."The History of the Shipping Companies of the Great Lakes."
    M.A. thesis, University of Toronto, 1929.

(Reprinted from Beeson's Marine Directory)

4 - DIRECTORIES AND REGISTERS

4-A.   NATIONAL AND INTERNATIONAL (Most Including Great Lakes)

American Bureau of Shipping. Record of American and Foreign Shipping.
    (Annual since 1867 when it was established by the American Ship-
    masters' Association as the Register of American and Foreign
    Shipping with title change to above in 1898.)

American Lloyds' Registry of American and Foreign Shipping. (Started in
    1857 as New York Marine Register, changed to American Lloyds' in
    1858 and continuing until about 1880 when absorbed by the Record
    of American and Foreign Shipping, above entry.)

Annals of Lloyds' Register. Being a sketch of the origin, constitution,
    and progress of Lloyd's Register of British and Foreign Shipping.
    London, 1884.

Blake, George. Lloyds' Register of Shipping 1760-1960. London: Lloyds'
    Register of Shipping, c. 1960.

Blue Book of American Shipping: Marine and Naval Directory of the United
    States. Cleveland: Marine Review Publishing Co. (Annual in the
    period c. 1895-1915.)

Canadian Ports and Seaway Directory. Gardenville, Quebec: National
    Business Publications. (Current annual since 1934.) (Name changed
    to Canadian Ports and Shipping Directory, 1934-1962.)

Canada, Department of Transport. Canada List of Shipping. Being a list of
    vessels on the registry books of the Dominion of Canada on the 31st
    December. Ottawa, Ontario: Edmond Cloutier. (Published annually
    c. 1886 to present under slightly different titles, publishers,
    and various government organizations.)

Lloyds' List 1741-1834. Reprint ed., England: Gregg International Pub-
    lishers, 1969.

Lloyds' Register of Shipping. Register of Ships. v. 1. London: Lloyds'
    Register of Shipping. (Current annual since 1834.)

_____. Appendix. v. 2. Register Book. London. (Current annual.)

_____. List of Shipowners. v. 3. Register Book. London. (Current
    annual.)

_____. Directory. v. 4. Register Book. Shipbuilders, docks, marine
    insurance underwriters, etc. London. (Current annual.)

Marine Engineering/Log. Marine Directory. New York: Simmons-Boardman
    Publishing Co. (Current annual.)

Society of Merchants, Ship-Owners, and Underwriters. The Register of
    Shipping. London: C. F. Seyfang, n.d.; reprint ed., London: Gregg
    Press, 1963. (Published from 1799-1834 and commonly known as the
    "Red Book.")

U. S. Treasury Department, Bureau of Navigation. List of Merchant Vessels
    of the United States. Washington. (Current annual since 1868.)
    (Government organization producing this series has varied over the
    years, e.g., Department of Commerce, Bureau of Navigation, 1916,
    and Treasury Department, Bureau of Customs, 1957, etc. Commonly
    referred to as simply "Merchant Vessels.")

4-B.   GREAT LAKES ONLY

Beeson's Marine Directory of the Northwestern Lakes. Chicago: Harvey C.
    Beeson. (Annual in the period 1888-1921 and published at various
    times in Detroit.)

Great Lakes Red Book. St. Clair Shores, Michigan: Fourth Seacoast Pub-
    lishing Co. (Current annual since 1902.   Originally published
    by Penton Publishing Co., Cleveland.)

Great Lakes Register. Cleveland: Bureau Veritas International Register of
    Shipping, 1896-1934. (Acquired and published by the American Bureau
    of Shipping from 1916 to 1934. Discontinued in 1935.)

Green's Great Lakes and Seaway Directory. North Olmsted, Ohio: M. E. Green.
    (Current annual since 1909.)

Greenwood, John O., and Dill, M. Greenwood's and Dill's Lake Boats.
    Clveland: Freshwater Press. (Current annual since 1965.)

Greenwood, John O. Greenwood's Guide to Great Lakes Shipping. Cleveland:
    Freshwater Press. (Current annual since 1960.)

Inland Lloyds Vessel Register. Buffalo: Art-Printing Works of Matthews,
   Northrup & Co. (c.1882-?). (Originally published as *Lake Vessel
   Register, System of Classification*. Buffalo: Board of Lake Under-
   writers (c. 1850 - c. 1880.)

Lynn's Marine Directory. Toronto: Lynn Publishing Co. (c. 1905 - c. 1919)
   (Some issues printed in Port Huron, Michigan.)

Manse, Thomas. *Know Your Ships: List of Vessels Passing Thru the United
   States and Canadian Locks*. 24th ed. Sault Ste. Marie, Michigan:
   Marine Publishing Co., 1982.

R. L. Polk and Company's Marine Directory of the Great Lakes. Detroit:
   R. L. Polk & Co., 1884, 1888, 1891.

Ship Masters' Association of the Great Lakes. Annual Directory of Names,
   Pennant Numbers and Addresses of All Members. Cleveland: Marine
   Review Print and various other printers or publishers for differ-
   ent editions. Name later changed to International Shipmasters'
   Association. 1893 to 1967.

Vessel Classification of the Inland Lloyds, Canadian Hulls. Toronto:
   Budget Printing & Publishing Co., 1882 and 1890.

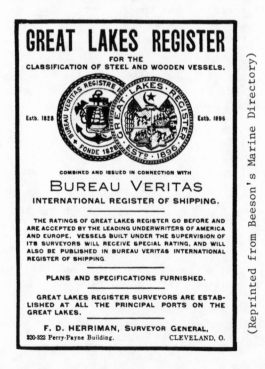

(Reprinted from Beeson's Marine Directory)

5-A.   *SHIPBUILDING ON THE LAKES*

Baker, Catherine C. Shipbuilding on the Saginaw. Bay City, Michigan:
     Museum of the Great Lakes, 1974; reprint ed., 1976.

Chicago Ship Building Company, Ship Builders and Engineers. Philadelphia:
     Armstrong and Fears, 1899.

Detroit Dry Dock Company. Around the Lakes. Detroit, 1894.

Gilkeson, Robert. Early Shipbuilding at Niagara. Niagara, Ontario: Niagara
     Historical Society, 1909.

"Great Lakes Engineering Works." International Marine Engineering 24
     (April 1919): 281-288.

Gregory, W. M. "Steel Shipbuilding on the Great Lakes." Geography and
     Industries of Cleveland 5 (1908).

Harold, Steve. Shipbuilding at Manistee. Manistee, Michigan: By the Author,
     1979.

Howland, Henry R. "Navy Island and the First Successors to the GRIFFON."
     Publications of the Buffalo Historical Society 6 (1903): 17-33.

Inches, H. C. The Great Lakes Wooden Shipbuilding Era. Cleveland: By the
     Author, 1962.

_____. "Wooden Ship Building." Inland Seas 7 (1951): 3-12.

Johnson, A. F. "New Shipbuilding Enterprise in Milwaukee." International
     Marine Engineering 24 (April 1919): 262-265.

"Lake Yards Set Record in Rapid Shipbuilding." Iron Trade Review 62
     (April 18, 1918): 997.

"Layout of Shipyard of Saginaw Shipbuilding Company." International
     Marine Engineering 24 (April 1919): 260-261.

"Manitowoc Shipbuilding Company." International Marine Engineering 24
    (April 1919): 271-280.

Marshall, O. H. The Building and Voyage of the GRIFFON in 1679. Buffalo:
    Bigelow Brothers, n.d.; reprint ed. from the Publications of the
    Buffalo Historical Society 1 (August 1870): 253-288.

Norton, Harold F. "Developments in Shipbuilding." Historical Transactions
    1893-1943. New York: Society of Naval Architects and Marine Engin-
    eers, 1945.

Pankhurst, J. F. "The Development of Shipbuilding on the Great Lakes."
    Transactions of the Society of Naval Architects and Marine Engin-
    eers 1 (1893): 252-262.

Remington, Cyrus Kingsbury. The Ship-Yard of the GRIFFON.   Buffalo: n.p.,
    1981.

Rosenberg, Max. The Building of Perry's Fleet on Lake Erie, 1812-1813.
    Harrisburg, Pennsylvania: Pennsylvania Historical and Museum
    Commission, 1950.

Smith, Andrew B. "Shipbuilding and Ship Repair on the Great Lakes." The
    American Merchant Marine 16 (September 27-29, 1950): 78-81. (Mid-
    century analysis proceedings of a conference on the American
    Merchant Marine sponsored by the Propeller Club of the United
    States in New York.)

True, Dwight. "Sixty Years of Shipbuilding." Paper presented at the Octobe
    5, 1956, meeting of the Great Lakes Section, Society of Naval
    Architects and Marine Engineers.

U. S. Shipping Board Emergency Fleet Corporation. "Armada of Steel Cargo
    Ships Built on the Lakes." Emergency Fleet News 1 (December 19,
    1918): 8.

U. S. Shipbuilding Labor Adjustment Board. Decision as to Wages, Hours and
    Other Conditions in Atlantic Coast, Gulf and Great Lakes Shipyards.
    Washington: Government Printing Office, 1918.

Vaughan, C. "Shipyards of the Great Lakes." Outlook 119 (July 3, 1918):
    381-382.

Wright, Richard J. Freshwater Whales: A History of the American Ship
    Building Company and Its Predecessors. Kent, Ohio: Kent State
    University, 1969; reprint ed., 1971.

5-B.   SHIP CONSTRUCTION METHODS

American Shipmasters' Association. Record of American and Foreign Shipping.
    New York: R. C. Root, Anthony & Co., 1872.

American Bureau of Shipping. 1902 Record of American and Foreign Shipping.
    New York: American Bureau of Shipping, 1902.

_____. Rules for Building and Classing Vessels. New York: American
    Bureau of Shipping, 1900.

_____. Rules for the Classification and Construction of Steel Vessels.
    New York: American Bureau of Shipping, 1968.

"Berth Construction and Side-Launching Practice in Great Lakes Shipyards."
    Engineering News 82 (January 2, 1919): 7-13.

Brewington, M. V. Shipcarvers of North America. New York: Dover Publica-
    tions, 1962.

Bureau Veritas International Register of Shipping. Rules and Regulations
    for the Building and Classification of Steel Vessels Intended for
    Inland Navigation. London: Bureau Veritas International Register of
    Shipping, 1913.

Curr, Robert. "Lake Ship Yard Methods of Steel Ship Construction." Marine
    Review 35 (May 30, 1907): 40-42.

Curtis, W. H. The Elements of Wood Ship Construction. New York: McGraw-
    Hill Book Co., 1919.

Dorr, E. P. Rules for Construction, Inspection and Characterization of
    Sail and Steam Vessels. Buffalo: By the Author, 1876.

Estep, H. Cole. How Wooden Ships are Built. Cleveland: Penton Publishing
    Co., 1918.

Fincham, John. A Treatise on Masting Ships and Mast Making. London:
    Whittaker & Co., 1843.

Gill, Claude S. Steel's Elements of Mastmaking, Sailmaking and Rigging.
    n.p., 1794; reprint ed., New York: Edward Sweetman, 1932.

"The Hull and Rig of Vessels." 19th Annual List of Merchant Vessels of
    the United States, for the Year Ended June 30, 1887. Washington:
    Government Printing Office, 1888.

Inland Lloyds. 1882 Vessel Classification of the Inland Lloyds' American
    Hulls. Buffalo: Printing House of Matthews, Northrup & Co., 1882.

Lloyds' Register of British and Foreign Shipping. Rules and Regulations
    for the Construction and Classification of Steel Vessels, from 1st
    July 1902, to the 30th June 1903. London: Lloyds' Register of
    British and Foreign Shipping.

Manitowoc Shipbuilding Company. Names of the Different Parts of a Ship,
    How a Ship is Built, Ship Building Trades. Manitowoc, Wisconsin:
    Manitowoc Shipbuilding Co., 1917.

_____. Fitters Hand Book. Manitowoc, Wisconsin: Manitowoc Shipbuilding
    Co., 1917.

McMyler Interstate Company. Shipbuilding Cranes. Cleveland: McMyler
    Interstate Co., 1919.

"Pre-Assembly System and Efficient Erection Cranes Speed Up Shipbuilding
    at Ecorse Yards of the Great Lakes Engineering Works." Engineering
    News 81 (December 12, 1918): 1076-1081.

Story, Dana A. The Building of a Wooden Ship. Barre, Massachusetts: Barre
    Publishers, 1971.

Underhill, Harold A. Masting and Rigging the Clipper Ship and Ocean
    Carrier. Glasgow: Brown, Son & Ferguson, 1946; reprint ed., 1969.

_____. Sailing Ship Rigs and Rigging: With Authentic Plans of Famous
    Vessels of the Nineteenth and Twentieth Centuries. Glasgow:
    Brown, Son & Ferguson, 1938; reprinted 1948.

The United States Standard Steamship Owners', Builders', and Under-
    writers' Association. The United States Standard Register of
    Shipping, with Rules for the Construction and Classification of
    Iron, Steel, Composite and Wooden Vessels, 1893-94. New York:
    United States Standard Steamship Owners', Builders', and Under-
    writers' Association, 1894.

5-C. MARINE ENGINEERING

Babcock and Wilcox Company. Marine Steam. New York: Babcock & Wilcox Co.,
    1928.

Baker, W. A. The Engine-Powered Vessel. Gothenburg, Sweden: Tre Tryckare,
    Cagner & Co., 1965.

Corkhill, Michael. The Tonnage Measurement of Ships: Towards a Universal
    System. London: Fairplay Publications, 1977.

Gilfillan, S. C. Inventing the Ship. Chicago: Follett Publishing Co.,
    1935.

Hyde, Charles E. "The Modern Marine Engine." Cassier's Magazine (August
    1897).

Main, Thomas. The Progress of Marine Engineering from the Time of Watt
    Until the Present Day. New York: Trade Publishing Co., 1893.

Ministry of Transport and Civil Aviation. Instructions As to the Tonnage
    Measurement of Ships. London: Her Majesty's Stationery Office,
    1953.

Nichols, John F. "The Development of Marine Engineering." Historical
    Transactions 1983-1943. New York: Society of Naval Architects &
    Marine Engineers, 1945.

Oldham, Joseph R. "Shipbuilding and Transportation on the Great American
    Lakes." Cassier's Magazine (August 1897).

Preble, George Henry. A Chronological History of the Origin and Development of Steam Navigation. 2nd ed. Philadelphia: L. R. Hamersly & Co., 1895. (An index to the names of vessels in the first edition [1883] of this work has been prepared by John L. Lockhead of Winthrop, Massachusetts, and was published as a manuscript by the compiler in 1942.)

Smith, Edgar C. A Short History of Naval and Marine Engineering. Cambridge, England: University Press, 1937.

U. S. Bureau of Navigation, Department of Commerce. Measurement of Vessels. 3rd ed. Washington: Government Printing Office, 1919. (Updated periodically.)

5-D.   MODEL SHIPBUILDING

Davis, Charles G. The Built-Up Ship Model. Salem, Massachusetts: Marine Research Society, 1933.

_____. The Ship Model Builder's Assistant. New York: Edward W. Sweetman Co., 1960.

Grimwood, V. R. American Ship Models and How to Build Them. New York: Bonanza Books, 1942.

Johnson, Gene. Ship Model Building. 3rd ed. Cambridge, Maryland: Cornell Maritime Press, 1961.

Porter, Kent. Building Model Ships from Scratch. Blue Ridge Summit, Pennsylvania: Tab Books, 1977.

Underhill, Harold A. Plank-On-Frame Models and Scale Masting and Rigging. 2 vols. Glasgow: Brownson & Ferguson, 1958.

6-A.   GENERAL SHIPWRECK HISTORY AND LORE

Ayre, John C., and Paulter, Ward. Shipwrecks. Buffalo: Niagara Frontier
  Underwater Society, 1978.

Barcus, Frank. Freshwater Fury. Detroit: Wayne State University Press,
  1960.

Barry, James P. Wrecks and Rescues of the Great Lakes: A Photographic
  History. LaJolla, California: Howell-North Books, 1981.

Bowen, Dana Thomas. Shipwrecks of the Lakes. Cleveland: Freshwater Press,
  1952.

Boyer, Dwight. Ghost Ships of the Great Lakes. New York: Dodd, Mead &
  Co., 1968.

Cochrane, Hugh F. Gateway to Oblivion: The Great Lakes' Bermuda Triangle.
  London: W. H. Allen, a Howard & Wyndham Co., 1980.

Fleming, Robert M. A Primer of Shipwreck Research and Records for Skin
  Divers, Including an Informal Bibliography Listing Over 300
  Sources of Shipwreck Information. Milwaukee: Global Manufacturing
  Corp., 1971.

Great Lakes Shipwrecks. Grand Marais, Michigan: Voyager Press, 1977;
  revised ed., 1978.

Haseltine, Curt. Great Heroism on the Great Lakes. Detroit: Freshwater
  Press, 1960.

Lloyd, James T. Lloyd's Steamboat Directory and Disasters on the Western
  Waters. Cincinnati: James T. Lloyd & Co., 1856. (Although con-
  cerned mostly with disasters on western rivers such as the
  Mississippi, this citation includes detailed information on nine
  major disasters on the Great Lakes--ERIE, PHOENIX, ATLANTIC,
  GRIFFITH, etc.)

Marx, Robert. Shipwrecks of the Western Hemisphere. New York: World
  Publishing Co., 1976.

Ratigan, William. Great Lakes Shipwrecks and Survivals. 3rd ed. Grand
    Rapids, Michigan: Wm. B. Eerdmans Publishing Co., 1981.

Reddeman, Chester C. "Great Lakes Shipwreck Study." Warren, Michigan:
    By the Author, (c. 1979).

"Shipwrecks on the Lakes." Michigan in Books 14 (Spring-Summer 1979): 3-
    18.

6-B.   *SHIPWRECKS BY GEOGRAPHIC AREA*

Amos, Art, and Folkes, Patrick. A Diver's Guide to Georgian Bay. Toronto:
    Ontario Underwater Council, 1979.

Engman, Elmer. Shipwreck Guide to the Western Half of Lake Superior.
    Booklet. Duluth: Innerspace, 1976.

Folkes, Patrick. Shipwrecks of Tobermory 1828-1935. Willowdale, Ontario:
    By the Author, 1969.

_____. Shipwrecks of the Saugeen 1828-1938. Willowdale, Ontario: By
    the Author, 1970.

Frederickson, Arthur C., and Lucy F. Ships and Shipwrecks in Door County,
    Wisconsin. 2 vols. Sturgeon Bay, Wisconsin: Door County Publishing
    Co., 1961 and 1963.

Frimodig, Mac. Shipwrecks Off Keweenaw. Published by the Fort Wilkins
    Natural History Association in cooperation with the Michigan
    Department of Natural Resources (c. 1975).

Hollister, Frederick F. "Shipwrecks of the Manitou Passage." Telescope
    17 (September-October 1968): 151-159.

Hulse, Charles Allen. "A Spatial Analysis of Lake Superior Shipwrecks:
    A Study in the Formative Process of the Archaeological Record."
    Ph.D. dissertation, Michigan State University, 1981.

Lane, Kit. Shipwrecks of the Saugatuck Area. Saugatuck, Michigan: Commercial Record, 1974.

_____. Some Stories of Holland Harbor. Saugatuck, Michigan: Commercial Record, 1975.

Opheim, Lee Alfred. "Twentieth Century Shipwrecks in Lake Superior." Ph.D. dissertation, St. Louis University, 1972.

Pitz, Herbert. Lake Michigan Disasters. Manitowoc, Wisconsin: Manitowoc Maritime Museum, 1925; reprint ed., (c. 1979).

Rowe, Alan R. Hollow Pits Sunken Ships: The Story of Wisconsin's Forgotten Stone Fleet. Milwaukee: Rowe Publications, 1979.

Salen, Rick, and Jack. The Tobermory Shipwrecks. Tobermory, Ontario: Mariner Chart Shop, 1976.

Stabelfeldt, Kimm A. Explore Wisconsin Shipwrecks. Milwaukee: Rowe Publications, 1981.

Stonehouse, Frederick. Great Wrecks of the Great Lake: A Directory of Shipwrecks of Lake Superior. Marquette, Michigan: Harboridge Press, 1973.

_____. Isle Royale Shipwrecks. 2nd ed. AuTrain, Michigan: Avery Color Studios, 1977.

_____. Went Missing: Fifteen Vessels That Disappeared on Lake Superior. 2nd ed. AuTrain, Michigan: Avery Color Studios, 1977.

_____. Marquette Shipwrecks. 2nd ed. AuTrain, Michigan: Avery Color Studios, 1978.

_____. Munising Shipwrecks. Marquette, Michigan: Shipwrecks Unlimited, 1980.

Warner, Thomas D., and Holecek, Donald F. The Thunder Bay Shipwreck Survey Study Report. Lansing, Michigan: Recreation Research and Planning Unit, Department of Park and Recreation Resources, Michigan State University, 1975.

Wolff, Julius F. The Shipwrecks of Lake Superior. Duluth: Lake Superior
   Marine Museum Association, 1979. (This book in part is based on
   numerous articles published by Wolff in Inland Seas.)

6-C.   SHIPWRECKS - SPECFIC VESSELS

Billow, Jack J. "The Tragedy of the EASTLAND." Inland Seas 16 (1960):
   190-195.

Busch, Gregory James. Lake Huron's Death Ship. Saginaw, Michigan: Busch
   Oceanographic Equipment Co., 1975. (The PEWABIC.)

Caesar, Pete C. 1880 Storm: ALPENA is Missing. Green Bay, Wisconsin:
   Great Lakes Maritime Research, 1980.

Craig, John. The NORONIC is Burning! Don Mills, Ontario: General Publishing Co., 1976.

Dowling, Rev. Edward J. "Tragedy at Clark Street Bridge." Steamboat Bill
   22 (1965); 43-49. (The EASTLAND.)

"EASTLAND Disaster and Vessel Stability." Engineering News 74 (September
   9, 1915): 516-517.

Engman, Elmer. In the Belly of a Whale. Booklet. Duluth: Innerspace, 1976.
   (The whaleback THOMAS WILSON.)

Hainault, Paul Edmund. The Singing Sirens that Sank the FITZ. Houghton,
   Michigan: By the Author, 1979.

Hemming, Robert J. Gales of November: The Sinking of the EDMUND FITZGER-
   ALD. Chicago: Contemporary Books, 1981.

Investigation of Accident to the Steamer EASTLAND Containing a Copy of
   Testimony and Report of Board of Inquiry Made to the Committee
   of Commerce. Also, Preliminary Report of the Committee of Super-
   visors and Inspectors of the Steamboat Inspection Service.
   Washington, 1916.

Kimball, F. D. The Great Collision Case. E. B. Ward, et. al. Owners of
the Steamer ATLANTIC, the Propeller OGDENSBURGH, and Chamberlain
and Crawford, Her Owners. Tried and Determined at Colombus in
the District of Ohio, U. S. District Court, 1853. Reported from
original minutes taken at the trial. Cleveland: Harris & Fair-
banks, 1853.

Lee, Robert E. EDMUND FITZGERALD 1957-1975. Detroit: Great Lakes Maritime
Institute, 1977.

Musham, Harry Albert. "Early Great Lakes Steamboats: Hard Times and the
ERIE Disaster, 1840-1841." The American Neptune 20 (1960): 79-103.

The Mystery Ship From 19 Fathoms. AuTrain, Michigan: Avery Color Studios,
1974. (The ALVIN CLARK.)

Scanlan, Charles M. The LADY ELGIN Disaster September 8, 1860. Milwaukee:
By the Author, 1928.

Scott, William Ellison. The Wreck of the LAFAYETTE. Two Harbors, Michigan:
Scott-Mitchell Publishing Co., 1959.

Stein, C. E. The Wreck of the ERIE BELLE. Wheatley, Ontario: Ship'n Shore
Publishing Co., 1970.

Stonehouse, Frederick. Wreck of the EDMUND FITZGERALD. AuTrain, Michigan:
Avery Color Studios, 1977.

Stover, Frances M. "The Schooner That Sunk the LADY ELGIN." Wisconsin
Magazine of History 7 (1924): 30-40.

Van Eyck, William O. "The Story of the Propeller PHOENIX." Wisconsin
Magazine of History 7 (1924): 281-300.

U. S. Coast Guard. Marine Board of Investigation: Sinking of the EDMUND
FITZGERALD 10 November 1975. Report No. USCG 16732/64216. Washington: July 26, 1977. (A complete transcript of the hearings
held by the Coast Guard is available at the Milwaukee Public
Library.)

Beeson's Marine Directory of the Northwestern Lakes. Chicago: Harvey C.
    Beeson, 1888-1921. (Contains an annual list of vessels lost.)

Berman, Bruce D. Encyclopedia of American Shipwrecks. Boston: Mariners
    Press, 1972.

Carus, Edward. "100 Year Span on Great Lakes Took Heavy Toll - 1831-
    1931." Manitowoc Herald News (November 19 and December 29,
    1931). (Contains an indexed Great Lakes wreck list.)

Davison, Robert H. Great Lakes Shipwreck List. Detroit: Maritime Research
    & Publishing, 1962.

Hall, Captain J. W., comp. Marine Disasters on the Western Lakes During
    the Navigation of 1871. Detroit: Free Press Book & Job Printing
    Establishment, 1872.

_____. Hall's Record of Lake Marine Embracing the Marine Casualties
    of 1877. Detroit: Wm. Graham's Steam Presses, 1878.

Heden, Karl E. Directory of Shipwrecks of the Great Lakes. Boston: Bruce
    Humphries Publishers, 1966.

Lonsdale, Ardian L., and Kaplan, H. R. A Guide to Sunken Ships in
    American Waters. Arlington, Virginia: Compass Publications, 1964.

Lynn's Marine Directory. Toronto: Lynn Publishing Co. (c. 1905-1919).

Lytle, William M., and Holdcamper, Forrest R., comp. Merchant Steam
    Vessels of the United States 1790-1868. "The Lytle-Holdcamper
    List." Staten Island, New York: Steamship Historical Society of
    American, 1952; revised and edited ed. by C. Bradford Mitchell
    and Kenneth R. Hall, 1975. (Includes Supplement No. 1, 1978.)

Mansfield, J. B. History of the Great Lakes v. 1. Chicago: J. H. Beers
    & Co., 1899; reprint ed., Cleveland: Freshwater Press, 1972.

Marine Casualties of the Great Lakes 1863-1873. Microfilm Publication
    No. T729. Washington: National Archives, n.d.

Mills, John M. Canadian Coastal and Inland Steam Vessels, 1809-1930.
    Providence, Rhode Island: Steamship Historical Society of America,
    1979. (Includes Supplement No. 1, 1981.)

_____. "Accidents and Damage to Vessels on the Great Lakes and Connec-
    ting Channels, 1901-1910." Manuscript, n.p., n.d.

"Preliminary Historical Inventory of Water Related Sites for Northern
    Ohio." (Location of Shipwrecks in Lake Erie.) Bowling Green, Ohio:
    Center for Archival Collections at Bowling Green State University.
    (Through a grant from the Ohio Coastal Zone Management Program.)
    (c. 1980.)

Runge, Herman G. "Runge Shipwreck Log 1679 to 1943." From the Herman G.
    Runge Collection Acquired by the Milwaukee Public Library in 1958.

Tumilty, Tom. Shipwrecks of the Great Lakes. Bramalea, Ontario: n.p.,
    1971.

U. S. Coast Guard. Accidents and Casualties to Vessels in the Tenth Coast
    Guard District for the Period July 1, 1908, to June 30, 1918.
    Washington: National Archives.

U. S. Coast Guard. Accidents and Casualties to Vessels in the Eleventh
    Coast Guard District for the Period July 1, 1908, to June 30,
    1918. Washington: National Archives.

U. S. Coast Guard. Accidents and Casualties to Vessels in the Twelfth
    Coast Guard District - West Side of Lake Michigan and Lake
    Superior, July 1, 1908, to June 30, 1918. Washington: National
    Archives.

U. S. Coast Guard. Index to U. S. Coast Guard Casualty and Wreck Reports,
    1913-39. Microfilm Publication No. T926. Washington: National
    Archives.

U. S. Coast Guard. Life Saving Service Reports of Assistance Rendered.
    (From Stations listed below:) Washington: National Archives.

    Ashtabula, 1894-1904, 1911-15 (2 vols.)
    Bailey's Harbor, 1896-1919 (3 vols.)
    Buffalo, 1883-1918 (11 vols.)
    Charlevoix, 1900-20 (4 vols.)
    Charlotte, 1889-1918 (8 vols.)

U. S. Coast Guard. Life Saving Service Reports of Assistance Rendered.
(Continued from previous page.)

Chicago, 1895-1902 (1 vol.)
Cleveland, 1883-1917 (11 vols.)
Crisps, 1885-1916 (1 vol.)
Duluth, 1895-1915 (20 vols.)
Erie, 1893-1917 (9 vols.)
Evanston, 1883-1917 (5 vols.)
Fort Niagara, 1893-1922 (4 vols.)
Grand Point Au Sable, 1883-1902 (1 vol.)
Holland, 1887-1936 (6 vols.)
Jackson Park, 1893-1916 (4 vols.)
Kenosha, 1883-1916 (4 vols.)
Lake View Beach, 1898-1915 (1 vol.)
Marquette, 1891-1921 (3 vols.)
Milwaukee, 1893-1920 (3 vols.)
Muskegon, 1880-1918 (4 vols.)
North Manitou, 1883-1921 (4 vols.)
Oswego, 1883-1916 (6 vols.)
Portage-Ship Canal, 1886-1918 (4 vols.)
Racine, 1883-1921 (8 vols.)
Sheboygan, 1883-1917 (4 vols.)
South Chicago, 1890-1921 (4 vols.)
Sturgeon Bay, 1898-1918 (4 vols.)
Thunder Bay, 1883-1916 (5 vols.)
Two Rivers, 1883-1920 (5 vols.)
Vermilion, 1886-1922 (2 vols.)

U. S. Coast Guard. Strandings Reported to Have Occurred on the Great
Lakes for the Ten Year Period 1928 to 1937. Washington: National
Archives.

U. S. Coast Guard. U. S. Coast Guard Casualty and Wreck Reports, 1913-39.
Microfilm Publicaton No. T925. Washington: National Archives.

U. S. Coast Guard. U. S. Coast Guard Reports of Assistance Rendered to
Individuals and Vessels, 1916-40. Microfilm Publication No. T920.
Washington: National Archives.

U. S. Corps of Engineers. "History of Accidents, Casualties and Wrecks on
Lake Superior 1847 to 1930 Inclusive." Unpublished manuscript in
Burton Historical Collections of the Detroit Public Library, by
Peter C. Bullard. Also known as the "Wells List" by Homer Wells.

U. S. Customs Service. Collectors of Customs Reports of Casualty from the Customs House Districts. (Listed below:) Washington: National Archives.
Chicago, 1879-95 (8 vols.)
Detroit, 1889-93 (1 vol.)
Duluth, 1874-1901 (2 vols.)
Erie, 1874-83 (1 vol.)
Milwaukee, 1874-99 (9 vols.)
Osewgatchie, 1874-1921

U. S. Department of Agriculture, Weather Bureau. Report of Wrecks Which Occurred on the Great Lakes from December 17, 1885, to November 15, 1893. Washington: National Archives, 1894.

U. S. Department of Agriculture, Weather Bureau. Wrecks and Casualties on the Great Lakes During 1895, 1896 and 1897, by Willis L. Moore and Norman B. Conger. Washington: National Archives, 1898.

U. S. Department of Commerce. U. S. Steamboat Inspection Service. Annual Report of the Supervising Inspector General. Washington: National Archives, 1872-1914. (From 1853 to 1871 occasional records are found in the Annual Report of the U. S. Treasury Department who had jurisdiction over the U. S. Steamboat Inspection Service until 1903. Reports vary from calendar year to fiscal year.) Also see page 55.

U. S. Life Saving Service."List of Marine Disasters in the District of Michigan,1863-73." Letter from the Grand Haven Collector of Customs, dated December 23, 1873. Life-Saving Letters Received 1 (1873) G18.

U. S. Life Saving Service. "Wrecks and Casualties to Vessels Which Have Occurred on the East Shore of Lake Michigan from 1878-83." Life-Saving Letters Sent - Disasters to Shipping 1 (1883): 393-417.

U. S. Life Saving Service. "Wrecks and Casualties to Vessels Which Have Occurred on the West Shore of Lake Michigan from 1878-83." Life-Saving Letters Sent - Disasters to Shipping 1 (1883): 418-479.

U. S. Life Saving Service. "Wrecks and Casualties to Vessels By Stranding South of Milwaukee, Wisconsin, and Grand Haven, Michigan, from 1879-89." Life-Saving Letters Sent - Disasters to Shipping 3 (1889): 289-294.

U. S. Lighthouse Board. "Report of Marine Disaster, Losses to Vessels, and Loss of Life on the Northern Lakes in 1848." Lighthouse Letter, Series P. 1849 (1849): 103-105.

U. S. Lighthouse Board. Abstract of Shipwrecks Occurring Near Light Station in the 10th and 11th Lighthouse Districts, 1872-73. Washington: National Archives.

U. S. Lighthouse Board. Light Station Reports of Shipwrecks. (From stations listed below:) Washington: National Archives.

Rock Island, 1873-1908	Kalamazoo, 1872-95
Two Harbors, 1913-14	North Point, 1874-75
Two Rivers, 1886-96	Presque Isle, 1879-1904
West Huron Island, 1898-1909	Port des Morts, 1863-1938
Alpena, 1890-1902	Pottowottamie, 1882-1911
Fair Haven, 1872-92	Rock of Ages, 1909-33

U. S. Revenue Cutter Service. Reports of Assistance Rendered from Vessels BIBB, 1882-89 and MACKINAC, 1906-15. Washington: National Archives.

U. S. Revenue Cutter Service. Abstracts of Reports of Assistance Rendered from Vessels FESSENDEN, 1886-95; JOHNSON, 1886-95; PERRY, 1886-95. Washington: National Archives.

U. S. Treasury Department, Bureau of Navigation. List of Merchant Vessels of the United States. Washington. (Current annual since 1868.) (Government organization producing this series has varied over the years, e.g., Department of Commerce, Bureau of Navigation, 1916, and Treasury Department, Bureau of Customs, 1957, etc. Commonly referred to as simply "Merchant Vessels." Contains a list of casualties after 1905.)

U. S. Treasury Department. U. S. Coast Guard. Annual Report. Washington. (Current annual since 1915.)

U. S. Treasury Department. U. S. Life-Saving Service. Annual Report for Fiscal Year July 1 to June 30. Washington, 1876-1914.

Vierthaler, Arthur A. Superior's Sunken Ships. Extracted from the Milwaukee Journal, January 10, 1965.

Winkelmann, A. Shipping Casualties Resulting in Total Loss on the Great
    Lakes From 1870 to 1970. (Canadian vessels only.) n.p., (c. 1978).

Wright, Richard J., comp. "Inventory of Shipwrecks Within Michigan
    Coastal Waters." Bowling Green, Ohio: Northwest Ohio Great Lakes
    Research Center and Michigan Department of Natural Resources in
    Lansing, (c. 1972).

6-E.   WRECK AND TREASURE CHARTS

Ackerman, Paul W. Lake Dive Charts: Principle Shipwrecks Located and
    Identified. (For the following Great Lakes.) Chicago: Midwest
    Explorers League. (Updated periodically.)

    Lake Erie, June 1981
    Lake Huron, January 1981
    Lake Michigan, September 1981
    Lake Michigan - South Shores, July 1979
    Lake Ontario, June 1980
    Lake Superior, January 1981

Coffman, F. L. Treasure Map of the Great Lakes. (Wreck chart.) Mackinaw
    City, Michigan: Algomah Insturment Co., 1952.

Frederickson, Arthur C., and Lucy F. Frederickson's Treasure Chart of
    Lost Ships and Cargoes in the Frankfort, Michigan, Area: 200
    Miles, 200 Ships, 2 Billion Dollars. (Wreck chart.) Frankfort,
    Michigan: By the Authors, 1957.

_____. Frederickson's Chart of Ships Wrecked in the Vincinity of Door
    County, Wisconsin. (Wreck chart.) Frankfort, Michigan: By the
    Authors, 1959.

_____. Frederickson's Chart of Ships Wrecked from Algoma to Milwau-
    kee, Wisconsin. (Wreck chart.) Frankfort, Michigan: By the
    Authors, 1961.

Hollister, Frederick F. Wreck Chart of North and South Manitou Islands.
    Yellow Springs, Ohio: n.p., 1967.

King, Ted. Lake Erie Wreck Chart. Cleveland: n.p., 1958.

Metzler, Gerald C. Lake Erie Shipwrecks (Map). Rocky River, Ohio: By
   the Author, 1978.

Salen, Rick and Jack. Southern Georgian Bay Shipwrecks. Tobermory,
   Ontario: Mariner Chart Shop, 1977.

Salen, Rick J. The Tobermory Shipwrecks. Tobermory, Ontario: Mariner
   Chart Shop, 1976.

Schultz, Gerald. Treasure Map of the Great Lakes Region. (Wreck chart)
   n.p., 1960.

_____. Guide to Treasure Map of the Great Lakes Region. n.p., 1961.

Terry, Thomas P. Great Lakes Treasure Wreck Atlas. LaCrosse, Wisconsin:
   Speciality Products, 1974.

U. S. Department of Agriculture, Weather Bureau. Meteorological Chart
   of the Great Lakes, Summary for the Season of 1900. v. 3., n.
   10, by Alfred J. Henry and Norman B. Conger. Washington: U. S.
   Department of Agriculture, Weather Bureau, 1901.

U. S. Department of Agriculture, Weather Bureau. Wreck and Casualty
   Chart of the Great Lakes, 1894. Washington: U. S. Department of
   Agriculture, Weather Bureau, 1895.

U. S. Department of Agriculture, Weather Bureau. Wreck Chart of the
   Great Lakes, from 1886 to 1891. Washington: U. S. Department of
   Agriculture, Weather Bureau.

Wise, Donald A., comp. A Descriptive List of Treasure Maps and Charts in
   the Library of Congress. 2nd ed. Washington: Library of Congress,
   1973.

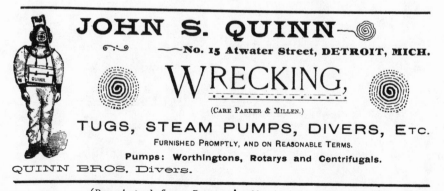
(Reprinted from Beeson's Marine Directory)

(Both as Author and Subject)

7-A.   U. S. CUSTOMS SERVICE

The primary source of information regarding the lineage of a vessel is
the complete set of Certificates of Enrollments for the vessel of
interest. In addition to the U. S. Customs House certificates of enrollment on microfilm (listed below) for Great Lakes vessels, individual
paper copies of original enrollment certificates may be obtained from
Record Group 41 of the National Archives and Records Service in Washington, D.C. Original copies of some certificates of enrollment are also
known to exist at the National Archives Regional Records Service Center
in Chicago and at various libraries scattered around the Great Lakes.
Certificates in these libraries (and other local Customs House records)
can usually be found listed in the manuscript card catalog. Paper copies
or certificates of enrollment and records of ownership for Canadian
vessels can be obtained from the Public Archives of Canada in Ottawa
(see Section 12-A).

Schmeckebier, Laurence F. The Customs Service, Its History, Activities
    and Organization. Monographs of the United States Government.
    No. 33. Baltimore: Johns Hopkins Press, 1924.

U. S. Customs Service. Certificates of Vessel Enrollments from Various
    Customs House Districts.(On microfilm as listed below.)
    Washington: National Archives

    Buffalo, 1816-96 (13 rolls)
    Chicago, 1847-66 (5 rolls)
    Cleveland, 1821-1911 (14 rolls)
    Detroit, 1818-98 (7 rolls)
    Green Bay, 1858-62; Manitowoc, 1863; Milwaukee,1851-68 (1 roll)
    Michilimackinac, 1831-63; Sault Ste. Marie,1847-68 (1 roll)
    Sandusky, 1857-66 (1 roll)
    Huron, Ohio, 1832; Portland, Ohio, 1823-46; Sandusky, 1847-1856
      (Partial roll, part of Sandusky 1816-1911 Master Abstracts of
      Enrollments.)

U. S. Customs Service. Collectors of Customs Reports of Casualty from
    the Customs House Districts. (Listed below.) Record Group 36.
    Washington: National Archives.

    Chicago, 1879-95 (8 vols.)
    Detroit, 1889-93 (1 vol.)
    Duluth, 1874-1901 (2 vols.)
    Erie, 1874-83 (1 vol.)
    Milwaukee, 1874-99 (9 vols.)
    Osewgatchie, 1874-1912 (1 vol.)

U. S. Customs Service. <u>Master Abstracts of Vessel Enrollments for Great
Lakes Customs House Districts.</u> (On microfilm as listed below.)
Washington: National Archives.

<u>ROLL NO. 1</u>
Sandusky, Ohio, 1816-1911

<u>ROLL NO. 2</u>
Detroit, 1816-17, 1839-1911
Michilimackinac and Sault Ste. Marie, 1833-68
Toledo, 1833-1911

<u>ROLL NO. 3</u>
Buffalo, 1822-1911
Cleveland, 1817-1911

<u>ROLL NO. 4</u>
Chicago, 1847-1911
Green Bay, 1846, 1859-60, 1864
Milwaukee, 1851-1911

<u>ROLL NO. 5</u>
(Overall 1815-1911. Several Custom Houses operated only for short
periods in this time frame.)

New York: Cape Vincent, Dunkirk, French Creek, Ogdensburg, Oswego,
Rochester, Sacketts Harbor, Suspension Bridge. Pennsylvania:
Presque Isle.

U. S. Treasury Department. U. S. Office of the Commissioner of Customs.
<u>Annual Report of the Commissioner of Customs.</u> Washington, 1853-?

Wright, Richard J., comp."Index to Great Lakes Customs House Vessel
Enrollments."(For Districts listed below.) Handwritten manuscript
available at the Center for Archival Collections, Bowling Green
State University, Bowling Green, Ohio, n.d.

Chicago, 1847-66
Detroit, 1815-64
Port Huron, 1866-71
Michilimackinac, 1833-68
Milwaukee, 1851-67

Short, Lloyd M. The Bureau of Navigation, Its History, Acitivites and Organization. Service Monographs of the United States Government. No. 15. Baltimore: Johns Hopkins Press, 1923.

U. S. Treasury Department. U. S. Bureau of Navigation. Annual Report of the Commissioner of Navigation. Washington, 1884-1932. (Department of Commerce and Labor, 1903-13, and Department of Commerce, 1913-32. Combined with Steamboat Inspection Service in 1932 to form Bureau of Navigation and Steamboat Inspection. Renamed Bureau of Marine Inspection and Navigation in 1936. Functions split in April 1942: vessel documentation to Bureau of Customs; remainder to U. S. Coast Guard. In 1968 all reunited in U. S. Coast Guard, then part of new Department of Transportation.)

7-C.   U. S. LIFE SAVING SERVICE

Bennett, Robert F. Surfboats, Rockets, and Carronades. Washington, Government Printing Office, 1976.

Ehrhardt, John. B. Joseph Francis (1801-1893) Shipbuilder, Father of the U. S. Life Saving Service. New York: Newcomen Society in North America, 1950.

Francis' Metallic Life-Boat Company. New York: William C. Bryant & Co., 1852.

Francis, J. A History of Life Saving Applicances Invented and Manufactured by Joseph Francis. N.p., 1885.

Kimball, Sumner I. Organization and Methods of the United States Life-Saving Service. Read before the Committee on Life-Saving Systems and Devices, International Marine Conference, 1889. Washington: Government Printing Office, 1894.

Law, W. H. Heroes of the Great Lakes. With an Account of the Recent Disasters. Detroit: Pohl Printing Co., 1906.

_____. The Life Savers in the Great Lakes. Incidents and Experiences Among the Life Savers in Lake Huron and Lake Superior Known as District 11. Detroit: Winn & Hammond, 1902.

Mason, Theodorus B. M. "The Preservation of Life at Sea." A paper read before the American Geographical Society. New York, 1879.

Noble, Dennis L., comp. United States Life-Saving Service Annotated Bibliography. Washington: U. S. Coast Guard Public Affairs Division, 1975.

O'Connor, William. Heroes of the Storm. Boston: Houghton, Mifflin & Co., 1904.

U. S. Coast Guard. Life Saving Service Reports of Assistance Rendered. (From stations listed below.) Washington: National Archives.

> Ashtabula, 1894-1904, 1911-15 (2 vols.)
> Bailey's Harbor, 1896-1919 (3 vols.)
> Buffalo, 1883-1918 (11 vols.)
> Charlevoix, 1900-20 (4 vols.)
> Charlotte, 1889-1918 (8 vols.)
> Chicago, 1895-1902 (1 vol.)
> Cleveland, 1883-1917 (11 vols.)
> Crisps, 1885-1916 (1 vol.)
> Duluth, 1895-1915 (20 vols.)
> Erie, 1893-1917 (9 vols.)
> Evanston, 1883-1917 (5 vols.)
> Fort Niagara, 1893-1922 (4 vols.)
> Grand Point Au Sable, 1883-1902 (1 vol.)
> Holland, 1887-1936 (6 vols.)
> Jackson Park, 1893-1916 (4 vols.)
> Kenosha, 1883-1916 (4 vols.)
> Lake View Beach, 1898-1915 (1 vol.)
> Marquette, 1891-1921 (3 vols.)
> Milwaukee, 1893-1920 (3 vols.)
> Muskegon, 1889-1918 (4 vols.)
> North Manitou, 1883-1921 (4 vols.)
> Oswego, 1883-1916 (6 vols.)
> Portage-Ship Canal, 1886-1918 (4 vols.)
> Racine, 1883-1921 (8 vols.)
> Sheboygan, 1883-1917 (4 vols.)
> South Chicago, 1890-1921 (4 vols.)
> Sturgeon Bay, 1898-1918 (4 vols.)
> Thunder Bay, 1883-1916 (5 vols.)
> Two Rivers, 1883-1920 (5 vols.)
> Vermilion, 1886-1922 (2 vols.)

U. S. Treasury Department. U. S. Life-Saving Service. Annual Report For Fiscal Year July 1-June 30. Washington, 1876-1914.

Short, Lloyd M. Steamboat-Inspection Service, Its History, Activities
    and Organization. Service Monographs of the United States
    Government. No. 8. New York: D. Appleton & Co., 1922.

U. S. Department of Commerce. U. S. Steamboat Inspection Service. Annual
    Report of the Supervising Inspector General. Washington, 1872-
    1914. (Also see page 47.)
    (Annual summaries of casualties investigated, 1853-1937.
        a) Appendix to printed Proceedings of the Board of Supervising
           Inspectors, 1853-94
        b) Appendix to printed Annual Report of the Steamboat Inspection
           Service, 1894-1915
        c) Transcript "Miscellanous Annual Reports of the Steamboat
           Inspection Service, etc, 1911-37
           - casualty investigation files of the Local Board of the
             Steamboat Inspection Service at Grand Haven, Michigan,
             1911-35
           - casualty reports of Eighth Supervising District (Detroit),
             1861-73
           - correspondence of the Steamboat Inspection Service, 1905-
             34. Contains some letters about and copies of investiga-
             tions of casualties.
    Bureau of Marine Inspection and Navigation Casualty Investigations,
    1937-42.)

7-E.   U. S. LIGHTHOUSE SERVICE

Conway, John S. The United States Lighthouse Service 1923. Washington:
    Department of Commerce, U. S. Lighthouse Service, 1923.

Holdcamper, Forrest R. Preliminary Inventory of the Field Records of the
    Lighthouse Service. Record Group 26. Washington: General Services
    Administration, National Archives and Records Service, The
    National Archives, 1964.

Johnson, Arnold Burges. The Modern Light-House Service. Washington:
    Government Printing Office, 1889.

Manning, Gordon P. Life in the Colchester Reef Lighthouse. Shelburne,
    Vermont: Shelburne Museum, 1958.

Noble, Dennis L., and O'Brien, T. Michael. Sentinels of the Rocks.
    Marquette, Michigan: Northern Michigan University Press, 1979.

Putnam, George R. Lighthouses and Lightships of the United States.
    Boston: Houghton Mifflin Co., 1917.

Secretary of the Treasury. U. S. Lighthouse Board. Annual Report of the
    Light-House Board. Washington, 1852-1910.

Secretary of the Treasury. U. S. Lighthouse Board. Report of the Officers
    Constituting the Light-House Board, to Inquire into the Condition
    of the Light-House Establishment of the United States, Under the
    Act of March 3, 1851. Washington: A. Boyd Hamilton, 1852.

Snow, Edward Rowe. Famous Lighthouses of America. New York: Dodd, Mead
    & Co., 1955.

Strobridge, Truman R. Chronology of Aids to Navigation and the Old
    Lighthouse Service 1716-1939. Washington: U. S. Coast Guard, 1974.

U. S. Coast Guard. Historically Famous Lighthouses. Publication CG-232.
    Washington: U. S. Coast Guard, Public Information Division,
    (c. 1980).

U. S. Commerce Department. U. S. Lighthouse Service. Annual Report of
    the Commissioner of Lighthouses. Washington, 1911-?

U. S. Light-House Board. Laws of the United States Relating to the
    Establishment, Support and Management of the Light-Houses, Light-
    Vessels, Monuments, Beacons, Spindles, Buoys and Public Piers of
    the United States from August 7, 1789 to March 3, 1855. Washing-
    ton: A. O. P. Nicholson, Public Printer, 1855.

U. S. Light-House Board. Light Station Reports of Shipwrecks. (From
    stations listed below.) Washington: National Archives.

        Rock Island, 1873-1908   Kalamazoo, 1872-95
        Two Harbors, 1913-14   North Point, 1874-75
        Two Rivers, 1886-96   Presque Isle, 1879-1904
        West Huron Island, 1898-1909   Port des Morts, 1863-1938
        Alpena, 1890-1902   Pottowottamie, 1882-1911
        Fair Haven, 1872-92   Rock of Ages, 1909-33

U. S. Light-House Board. Organization and Duties of the Light-House
    Board: And Rules, Regulations and Instructions of the Light-
    House Establishment of the United States with the Laws and Cir-
    culars Relating Thereto. Washington: Government Printing Office,
    1869.

U. S. Light-House Establishment. Compilation of Public Documents and Extracts from Reports and Papers Relating to Light-Houses, Light-Vessels, and Illuminating Apparatus, and to Beacons, Buoys and Fog Signals, 1789 to 1871. Washington: Government Printing Office, 1871.

U. S. Light-House Establishment. Instructions to Light Keepers. Washington: Government Printing Office, 1881 and 1902.

Weiss, George. The Lighthouse Service, Its History, Activities and Organization. Service Monographs of the United States Government. No. 40. Baltimore: Johns Hopkins Press, 1926.

7-F.   U. S. REVENUE CUTTER SERVICE

U. S. Revenue Cutter Service. Abstracts of Reports of Assistance Rendered. (From Vessels FESSENDEN, 1886-95; JOHNSON, 1886-95; PERRY, 1886-95.) Washington: National Archives & Records Service.

U. S. Revenue Cutter Service. Reports of Assistance Rendered. (From Vessels BIBB, 1882-89; MACKINAC, 1906-15.) Washington: National Archives & Records Service.

7-G.   U. S. COAST GUARD

Evans, Stephen H. The U. S. Coast Guard, 1790-1915, A Definitive History. Annapolis, Maryland: U. S. Naval Institute, 1949.

Holdcamper, Forrest R. Preliminary Inventory of the Records of the United States Coast Guard. Record Group 26. Washington: General Services Administration, National Archives and Records Service, National Archives, 1963.

Nalty, Bernard C., Noble, Dennis L., and Strobridge, Truman R. Wrecks, Rescues and Investigations: Selected Documents of the U. S. Coast Guard and Its Predecessors. Wilmington: Delaware: Scholarly Resources, 1978.

O'Brien, T. Michael. Guardians of the Eighth Sea: A History of the U. S. Coast Guard on the Great Lakes. Washington: U. S. Coast Guard, 1976.

Smith, Darrell H., and Powell, Fred Wilbur. The Coast Guard, Its History, Activities and Organization. Service Monographs of the United States Government. No. 51. Washington: Brookings Institution, 1929.

Strobridge, Truman, comp. United States Coast Guard Annotated Bibliography. Washington: U. S. Coast Guard Public Affairs Division, 1975.

U. S. Coast Guard. Index to U. S. Coast Guard Casualty and Wreck Reports, 1913-39. Microfilm Publication T926. Washington: National Archives.

U. S. Coast Guard. Light List: Volume IV Great Lakes (United States and Canada). Washington: Government Printing Office. (Current Annual.)

U. S. Coast Guard. U. S. Coast Guard Casualty and Wreck Reports, 1913-39. Microfilm Publication T925. Washington: National Archives.

U. S. Coast Guard. U. S. Coast Guard Reports of Assistance Rendered to Individuals and Vessels, 1916-40. Microfilm Publication T920. Washington: National Archives.

U. S. Coast Guard. U. S. Treasury Department. Annual Report. Washington, 1915 to present.

7-H.   OFFICE OF CHIEF OF ENGINEERS (CORPS OF ENGINEERS)

Corps of Engineers, United States Army. The United States Lake Survey. Detroit: United States Lake Survey, 1939.

Holt, W. Stull. The Office of the Chief of Engineers of the Army, Its Non-Military History, Activities and Organization. Service Monographs of the United States Government. No. 27. Baltimore: Johns Hopkins Press, 1923.

Larson, John. Essayons: A History of the Detroit District, U. S. Army
    Corps of Engineers. Washington: Government Printing Office, 1981.

_____. Those Army Engineers. A History of the Chicago District, U. S.
    Army Corps of Engineers. Washington: Government Printing Office,
    1981.

U. S. Lake Survey. Catalogue of Charts of the Great Lakes. Detroit: U.
    S. Lake Survey Office, 1939.

War Department. U. S. Engineer Department. Corps of Engineers. Annual
    Report of the Chief of Engineers. Washington, 1866 to present.

Woodfond, Arthur. (New history of U. S. Lake Survey in process by the
    Government Printing Office.)

7-I.   U. S. WEATHER SERVICE

Weber, Gustavus A. The Weather Bureau, Its History, Activities and
    Organization. Service Monographs of the United States. No. 9.
    New York: D. Appleton & Co., 1922.

7-J.   U. S. NAVY

(Also see Section 2-C-4.)

Chapelle, Howard. The American Sailing Navy. New York: W. W. Norton &
    Co., 1949.

Cooper, James Fenmore. A History of the Navy of the United States of
    America. New York: Stringer & Townsend, 1856.

Cuthbertson, George A. Freshwater. Montreal: Canada Steamship Lines,
    1923.

Nesser. R. W. Statistical and Chronological History of the United States Navy, 1775-1907. 2 vols. N.p., 1909.

Snider, C. H. J. In the Wake of the Eighteen-Twelvers. Toronto: Bell & Cockburn, 1913.

(Reprinted from Beeson's Marine Directory)

(For Wreck and Treasure Charts See 6-E)

8-A. GENERAL INFORMATION

Canada. Public Archives. Catalogue of the Maps, Plans and Charts in the Map Room of the Dominion Archives. Ottawa: Government Printing Bureau, 1912.

Carrington, David K., and Stephenson, Richard W. Map Collection in the United States and Canada. New York: Special Libraries Association, 1978.

Comstock, C. B. Annual Report Upon the Survey of Northern and Northwestern Lakes. Annual Report of the Chief of Engineers for 1874. Appendix CC.

Corps of Engineers, United States Army. The United States Lake Survey. Detroit: United States Lake Survey, 1939.

Department of Commerce and Department of Defense. Chart No. 1, United States of America, Nautical Chart Symbols and Abbreviations. 6th ed. Washington: National Ocean Survey, 1975.(Updated periodically.)

Department of Natural Resources, State of Michigan. Michigan Statewide Aerial Photography: Index Maps for the Upper and Lower Peninsulas. Lansing, Michigan: Department of Natural Resources, 1980.

Dunlap, G. D., and H. H. Shufeldt. Dutton's Navigation and Piloting. 12th ed. Annapolis, Maryland: U. S. Naval Institute, 1972.

Guide to Cartographic Records in the National Archives. Washington: National Archives Records Center, 1971.

Johnson, Edwin F. The Navigation of the Lakes. Hartford, Conneticut: Press of Case, Lockwood & Co., 1866.

Karpinski, Louis C. Bibliography of the Printed Maps of Michigan 1804-1880. Lansing, Michigan: Michigan Historical Commission, 1931; reprint ed., Amsterdam: Meridan Publishing Co., 1977

Karrow, Robert W., Jr., ed. Checklist of Printed Maps of the Middle West to 1900. Boston: G. K. Hall & Co., 1981. (Includes a series of volumes by region and/or State. v. 1, North Central States Region v. 2, Ohio; v. 3, Indiana; v. 4 Illinois; v. 5, Michigan; v. 6, Wisconsin; v. 7, Minnesota.)

Lloyd, Christopher. Atlas of Maritime History. New York: Hamlyn Publishing Group, 1975.

Maps of Michigan and the Great Lakes 1545-1845. Detroit: Burton Historical Collection, Detroit Public Library, n.d.

Meade, George G. Report of the Survey of the North and Northwest Lakes. Being Part of the Report of the Chief Topographical Engineer, Accompanying Annual Report of the Secretary of War, 1860. Detroit Daily Free Press Steam Printing House, 1861.

Muehrcke, Phillip C., and Juliana O. Map Use; Reading, Analysis and Interpretation. Madison, Wisconsin; J. P. Publications, 1978.

Plumb, Ralph G. History of Navigation of the Great Lakes. 61st Congress, 3rd Session, House Committee on Railways and Canals. Washington, 1887.

Ristow, Walter W. World Directory of Map Collections. Munich: Verlag Dokumentation, 1976.

Severance, Frank H., ed. "Journal of a Survey of the South Shore of Lake Erie Made in 1789." Publications of the Buffalo Historical Society 7 (1904): 365-376.

U. S. Lake Survey. Catalogue of Charts of the Great Lakes. Detroit: U. S. Lake Survey Office, 1939. (Updated periodically.)

For a complete list of current Great Lakes Navigation Charts, contact:

U. S. Waters:
Distribution Division (C44), National Ocean Survey, Riverdale, Maryland 20840 (301/436-6990)

Canadian Waters:
Chart Distribution Office, Department of the Environment, P. O. Box 8080, Ottawa, Ontario K1G 3H6 (613/998-4931)

Aside from the finding guides listed in Section 8-A, there is no single source the researcher can go to for a complete list of hydrographic maps of the Great Lakes by the U. S. Government.

By way of background, the Corps of Topological Engineers was created by an Act of congress in 1813. In 1831 they were made a distinct and independent bureau of the War Department. In 1839 Congress made all in-land river and harbor work solely that of the Corps of Topological Engineers, and by 1841 the U. S. Lake Survey had been established by the Corps and was first headquartered in Buffalo. In 1852 the Corps of Top-ological Engineers were given the survey work for all of the Great Lakes (not just rivers and harbors). About this time the U. S. Lake Survey was moved to Detroit and began to produce the first hydrographic maps for navigation on the Great Lakes. In 1863 the duties and work of the Corps of Topological Engineers were absorbed into the Corps of Engineers of the War Department. The U. S. Lake Survey was continued as an entity of the Corps of Engineers. They (U. S. Lake Survey, Detroit) continued to produce hydrographic maps until 1970 when they were merged with the U.S. Coast and Geodetic Survey to form the National Ocean Survey which is a division of the National Oceanic and Atmospheric Administration (NOAA). When this merger occurred, the U. S. Lake Survey Office in Det-roit was closed and its records were divided amongst the Library of Congress, the National Archives and the National Ocean Survey, making it very difficult to track information. The 1861 Meade report and the 1874 Comstock report listed in Section 8-A are excellent sources of informa-ion. Additionally, the U. S. Lake Survey periodically (and still does today) published Chart Indexes such as:

Corps of Engineers, U. S. Lake Survey. Index Chart of the Northern and Northwestern Lakes. Detroit: U. S. Lake Survey, 1885.

These indexes are extremely useful in determining the dates of publica-tion of different editions of a map of a given area. However, the chart numbering system changed several times making it difficult to establish a complete list of maps for one area.

Aside from the Library of Congress, the National Archives and the National Ocean Survey, almost all libraries around the Great Lakes have some sort of hydrographic map collection. Because the U. S. Lake Survey was located in Detroit, the best collections are in local Detroit-area libraries, e.g., the Burton Historical Collection of the Detroit Public Library, the University of Michigan Library in Ann Arbor, etc. The Burton Historical Collection, for example, has a special section of their card catalog (two drawers) devoted specifically to Great Lakes hydro-graphic maps. The collection at the Milwaukee Public Library is fair. We are sure that many other libraries (Cleveland, Buffalo, Toronto, etc.) have equally good collections, although we have not personally investiga-ted them.

With the background given above, the individual researcher is left to his or her own resourcefulness to locate the map of their own interest.

Barnet, James. Barnet's Coast Pilot for the Lakes. 4th ed. Chicago:
    By the Author, 1867. (See Thompson, Thomas S. below. This ed.
    is the first authored by Barnet alone after his split with
    Thompson c. 1863. Barnet published a 6th, 7th and 8th ed. inde-
    pendent of Thompson in 1872, 1874 and 1887.)

Canada, Department of Marine and Fisheries. Catalog of Marine Charts,
    Sailing Directions and Tidal Information. Ottawa: F. A. Ackland
    King's Printer, 1931.

Department of Transportation. U. S. Coast Guard. Coast Guard Radio Navi-
    gation Bulletin. Washington: Department of Transportation. (June
    1980 to present.)

Lin Leslie Y. Maggie's Drawers Are Coming Down - and Radio Takes Over.
    Booklet. Ann Arbor, Michigan: Michigan Sea Grant Program, n.d.

Minister of Marine and Fisheries. Georgian Bay and North Channel Pilot.
    Ottawa, Ontario: Government Printing Bureau, 1899.

Montague, C. M., ed. Great Lakes Waterway Guide. Grand Rapids, Michigan:
    Great Lakes Publishing Co. (Current annual since 1958.)

_____. Yachtsman's Guide to the Great Lakes. Grand Rapids, Michigan:
    Seaport Publishing Co. (Current annual since 1967.)

Monthly Bulletin of Lake Levels for the Great Lakes. Detroit: Department
    of the Army, Detroit District, Corps of Engineers. (Current.)

Scott, George. Scott's New Coast Pilot for the Lakes. 1st ed. Detroit:
    Detroit Free Press Book and Job Printing House, 1886. (2nd, 3rd,
    4th, 5th, 6th, 7th and 8th eds. published in 1888, 1890, 1892,
    1899, 1901, 1906 and 1914 respectively with five supplements
    issued in various intervening years.)

Strobridge, Truman R. Chronology of Aids to Navigation and the Old
    Lighthouse Service 1716-1939. Washington: U. S. Coast Guard, 1907.

Thompson, Thomas S. Thompson's Coast Pilot for the Upper Lakes. 1st ed.
    Chicago: James Barnet, 1859. (2nd and 3rd eds. also published by
    Barnet in 1861 and 1863. 4th, 5th and 6th eds. authored by
    Thompson and published in Detroit by Detroit Free Press Books and
    Job Printing House in 1865, 1869 and 1878 respectively.)

Transport Canada, Coast Guard. Notices to Mariners. Ottawa, Ontario:
    Aids & Waterways, Canadian Coast Guard. (Current annual.)

Trimble, Captain George, comp. The Lake Pilot's Handbook. Port Huron,
    Michigan: Riverside Printing Co., 1907.

U. S. Coast Guard. Light List: Volume IV Great Lakes (United States and
    Canada). Washington: Government Printing Office. (Current annual.)

U. S. Department of Commerce. National Oceanic and Atmospheric Adminis-
    tration, National Ocean Survey. Great Lakes Water Levels, 1860-
    1970. Detroit: Lake Survey Center, 1971.

U. S. Department of Commerce. United States Great Lakes Pilot, Washington:
    National Oceanic & Atmospheric Administration. (1964 to present.)

War Department, Corps of Engineers. Survey of Northern and Northwestern
    Lakes. Bulletin No. 1. Detroit: U. S. Lake Survey Office, 1891.
    (Numbers 1 to 70 published periodically from 1891 to 1963. Renamed
    Great Lakes Pilot in 1964.)

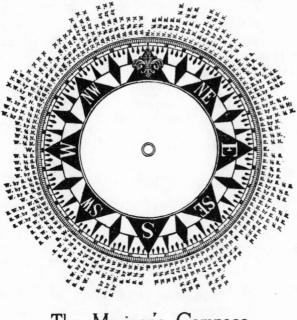

The Mariner's Compass

(Reprinted from Trimble's Lake Pilot's Handbook)

9-A.   MARINE NEWSPAPERS

American Shipbuilder (Weekly). New York: Bradley & Howell, est. 1890.

Canadian Shipping and Marine Engineering (Monthly). Mississauga,
     Ontario,1912 to present.

Great Lakes Commission. Great Lakes Newsletter (Monthly). Ann Arbor,
     Michigan: Institute of Science & Technology , 1956 to present.

Great Lakes Review (Monthly). Magazine of the Great Lakes Shipping
     Industry. Cleveland: Anthony J. Shylo, 1940 to present.

International Joint Commission. The Great Lakes Notebook (Monthly).
     Windsor, Ontario: Great Lakes Regional Office Information Ser-
     vices (Current).

Marine Engineering/Log (Monthly). New York, 1878 to present.

The Marine Journal (Weekly). New York, established 1878.

Marine Record (Weekly). Cleveland: Smith & Swainson, 1878-1902. (The
     official newspaper of the Lake Carriers' Association and the
     Cleveland Vessel Owners' Association.)

Marine Review. v. 1-65, March 6, 1890-October 1935. Cleveland: Penton
     Publishing Co. (Weekly March 6, 1890-March 25, 1909; Monthly
     April 1909-October 1935.) Absorbed the Marine Record in 1902.
     Marine Review merged into Marine Engineering and Shipping Age in
     1935, which merged into the Marine Engineering/Log.

The New York Maritime Register (Weekly). New York, established 1878.

Seabord (Weekly). New York: Smith & Stanton (c. 1895).

Seaway Review (Quarterly). Harbor Island, Maple City Postal Station,
     Michigan: LesStrang Publishing Co. (Current).

Shipping Register and Shipbuilder (Monthly). Montreal: Arco Press
     (Current).

Several finding guides for newspapers, primarily in microform, are listed in the following pages. These are followed by a listing of newspapers from major port cities which generally contained significant marine news.

The most extensive finding guides are those by the Library of Congress (they also publish a foreign version which contains Canadian listings) and it indicates libraries around the country where copies are available. For the State of Michigan the guide by the State Library contains only the holdings of that single library. Although this collection is extensive (988 newspapers from 237 Michigan cities), it by no means represents the holdings of all of Michigan libraries. Although we have not thoroughly yet checked, it is possible that other individual states have programs and guides similar to Michigan.

A large number of newspapers have not yet been microfilmed and exist only in original form. For example, the Burton Historical Collection of the Detroit Public Library is the only location to my knowledge which has nearly a complete collection of the Cheboygan Tribune and the Cheboygan Democrat in original form prior to 1900. This situation exists for many other newspapers, and I am not aware of any up-to-date finding guides for this material. The researcher is forced to determine if such material exists by checking with the library the researcher supposes most likely has it.

The city newspaper problem is further complicated by the many mergers and changes in name of any given newspaper. An example is shown in the illustration which immediately follows this narrative. The example chosen represents a case where the newspaper(s) in question generally carried an excellent marine column from a very early date, yet it went through many mergers and name changes. In the listing of city newspapers that follow, we have selected a few major port cities only as examples. In many cases the multiple listings represent basically a single newspaper that has gone through mergers and name changes. By studying the Library of Congress catalogs, the researcher can reconstruct his or her own newspaper genealogy diagram. Until someone publishes genealogy charts like that shown in our illustration, the researchers are left to their own devices (and the individual library card catalog) and the finding guides to figure out what newspaper name they should look under for the date of interest.

GENEALOGY OF A NEWSPAPER

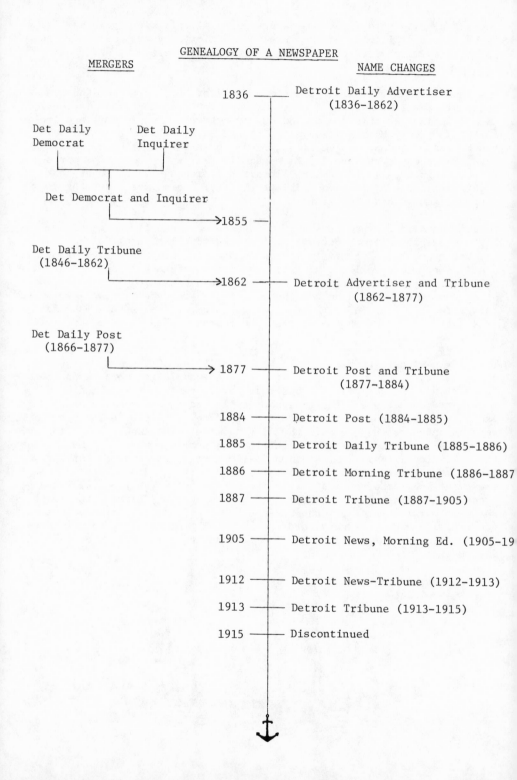

Gregory, Winifred, ed. American Newspapers 1821-1936. A Union List of
      Files Available in the United States and Canada. New York:
      Bibliographical Society of America, 1937; reprint ed., Kraus
      Reprint Corp., 1967.

Gutgesell, Stephen. Guide to Ohio Newspapers. Colombus: Ohio Historical
      Society, 1974.

Library of Congress Catalogs. Newspapers in Microform, United States,
      1948-1972 and 1973-1977. Washington: Library of Congress, 1977.
      (Foreign editions also available.)

Michigan Newspapers on Microfilm. 6th ed. Lansing, Michigan: Michigan
      State Board of Education, State Library, 1980.

Milner, Anita Cheek. Newspaper Indexes: A Location and Subject Guide for
      Researchers. 3 vols. Metuchen, New Jersey: Scarecrow Press, 1977-
      82.

Milwaukee Sentinel Index, 1837 to 1890. Milwaukee: Milwaukee Public
      Library, Local History Room.

Newspapers Available at Chicago Historical Society. Chicago: Chicago
      Historical Society, 1981.

New York Times Index. Quarterly, 1913-29; Annual, 1930 to present. New
      York: New York Times.

Scott, Franklin William. Newspapers and Periodicals of Illinois, 1814-
      1879. Springfield, Illinois: n.p., 1910.

Union List of Canadian Newspapers Held by Canadian Libraries. Ottawa:
      Newspaper Section, Services Division, Public Service Branch,
      National Library of Canada, 1977.

SAMPLE LISTING OF NEWSPAPERS OF MAJOR PORT CITIES:

1. Buffalo
    Buffalo Courier (1862-1926)
    Buffalo Courier-Express (1926-present)
    Buffalo Express (1860-1926)
    Buffalo Morning Express (1846-1855)
    Buffalo Morning Express and Daily Democrat (1855-1859)

2. Chicago
    Chicago Daily News (1875-1878)
    Chicago Daily Tribune (1847-1858)
    Chicago Herald (1914-1918)
    Chicago Herald and Examiner (1918-1939)
    Chicago Press and Tribune (1858-1860)
    Chicago Record-Herald (1901-1914)
    Chicago Record-Herald and Inter-Ocean (1914)
    Chicago Times (1861-1895)
    Chicago Times-Herald (1895-1901)
    Chicago Tribune (1860-present)
    Inter-Ocean (1872-1914)

3. Cleveland
    Cleveland Daily Plain Dealer (1845-1886)
    Cleveland Herald
    Cleveland Leader (1853-1917)
    Cleveland Plain Dealer   (1887-present)
    Cleveland Press (1885-present)
    Cleveland Penny Press (1878-1885)

4. Detroit
    Detroit Daily Advertiser, et al, 1836 ff (see illustration on page 68).
    Detroit Free Press
    -Detroit Daily Free Press (1835-1842)
    -Democratic Free Press (1842-1848)
    -Detroit Free Press (1848-1851)
    -Detroit Daily Free Press (1851-1858)
    -Detroit Free Press (1858-present)
    Detroit News
    -Evening News (1873-1905)
    -Detroit News (1905-1960)
    -Detroit Times (1904-1960, merged with Detroit News)
    -Detroit News and Times (1960 - ?)

5. Duluth
    Duluth Daily Tribune (1873-1892)
    Duluth News-Tribune (1893-present)
    Duluth Minnesotian, Duluth Minnesotian-Herald, Duluth Evening Herald,
    Duluth Herald (1869-present)

6. Milwaukee
    Milwaukee Sentinel and Gazette, Milwaukee Sentinel (1837-present)
    Milwaukee Journal
    -Daily Journal (1882-1883)
    -Milwaukee Daily Journal (1883-1890)
    -Milwaukee Journal (1890-present)

7. New York Times (1851-present)

8. Toronto
    Toronto Globe (1844-1869)
    Toronto Mail (1872-1880)
    Toronto Daily Mail (1880-1895)
    Toronto Evening Telegram

9-C.   *JOURNALS AND PERIODICALS*

The American Neptune (Quarterly journal). Salem, Massachusettes:
        Peabody Museum of Salem, 1941 to present.

Anchor News (Bi-monthly newsletter). Manitowoc, Wisconsin: Manitowoc
        Maritime Museum, 1975 to present.

The Bulletin. (Printed periodically during the shipping season.)
        Cleveland: Lake Carriers' Association, 1911 to present.

The Chadburn (Quarterly newsletter). Cleveland: Great Lakes Historical
        Society, H. H. Baxter, 1973 to present.

The Detroit Marine Historian (Monthly newsletter). Detroit: Marine
        Historical Society of Detroit, 1946 to present.

Great Lakes Gazette (Monthly newsletter). Grand Marais, Michigan:
        Voyager, People & Places, 1970 to present.

The Great Lakes Shipwreck Quarterly (Quarterly newsletter). Sault Ste.
        Marie, Michigan: Great Lakes Shipwreck Historical Society, 1980
        to present.

Inland Seas (Quarterly journal). Cleveland: Great Lakes Historical
     Society, 1945 to present.

Institute of Marine Engineers. First Volume of Transactions Comprising
     the Papers Published and Meetings Held During Session, 1889-90.
     Stratford, England: Langthorne Rooms, 1889-1972.

Lake Log Chips (Newsletter: Weekly, v. 1-9; Bi-weekly, v. 10 to present).
     Bowling Green, Ohio: Center for Archival Collections, March 14,
     1972 to present.

The Lightship (Monthly newsletter). Port Huron, Michigan: Lake Huron
     Lore Marine Society, 1980 to present.

Nor'Easter (Quarterly newsletter). Duluth: Lake Superior Marine Museum
     Association, 1976 to present.

Scanner (Monthly newsletter). Toronto: Toronto Marine Society.

Soundings (Quarterly magazine). Milwaukee: Wisconsin Marine Historical
     Society, 1959 to present.

Steamboat Bill (Quarterly journal). Providence, Rhode Island: Steamship
     Historical Society of America, 1940 to present.

Telescope (Six times per year, magazine). Detroit: Great Lakes Maritime
     Institute, 1952 to present.

(Reprinted from Beeson's Marine Directory)

The collections listed in this section are grouped first in alphabetical order by State and are arranged alphabetically within each State by the name of the holder of the collection. The number in parantheses after the collection name lists the approximate number of photographs or nega- tives in the collection. The listing is incomplete as some public libr- aries, historical societies and personal collections have not yet res- ponded with the appropriate detail.

10-A. INSTITUTIONAL AND COMMERCIAL

ILLINOIS

Great Lakes Graphics Collection (630). Great Lakes Graphics, Box 42654, Chicago, IL 60642.

IOWA

Steamboat Pictures and Documents (6,000). Davenport Public Museum, 704 Brady St., Davenport, IA 52804.

MARYLAND

The Steamship Historical Society of America Collection (30,000). Reference Librarian, Steamship Historical Society of America, University of Baltimore Library, 1420 Maryland Ave., Baltimore, MD 21201.

MICHIGAN

Burton Historical Photo Collection. Detroit Public Library, Burton His- torical Collection, 5201 Woodward, Detroit, MI 48202

Dossin Great Lakes Photo Collection (60,000). Dossin Great Lakes Museum, Detroit, MI 48207.

Rev. Edward J. Dowling Collection. Rev. Edward J. Dowling, Lansing Reilly Hall, University of Detroit, 4001 W. McNichols, Detroit, MI 48221.

Great Lakes Photo Collection. Marine Historical Society of Detroit, 877 University Place, Grosse Pointe, MI 48230.

Great Lakes Vessel Picture Collection (260). Museum of Arts and History
    1115 Sixth St., Port Huron, MI 48060.

Sailing Vessels from the Captain H. C. Inches Memorial Collection of
    Wooden Ships (350). Lake Huron Lore Society, Museum of Arts
    and History, 1115 Sixth St., Port Huron, MI 48060.

Munson Collection. State of Michigan Library Services, 735 E. Michigan
    Ave., Lansing, MI 48909.

MINNESOTA

Great Lakes Photo Collection. Canal Park Museum, U. S. Army Corps of
    Engineers, Duluth, MN 55802

NEW YORK

Great Lakes Photo Collection. Buffalo and Erie County Historical Society,
    25 Nottingham Court, Buffalo, NY 14216.

The New York Public Library Collection. Photoduplication Services, New
    York Public Library, 5th Ave. & 42nd St., New York, NY 10018.

OHIO

Freshwater Press Collection (418). Freshwater Press, Inc., P. O. Box
    14009, Cleveland, OH 44114.

Great Lakes Historical Society Picture Collection (10,000). Great Lakes
    Historical Society, 480 Main St., Vermilion, OH 44089.

Great Lakes Picture Collection (150,000). Center for Archival Collections,
    5th Floor, University Library, Bowling Green State University,
    Bowling Green, OH 43403.

VIRGINIA

The Mariners Museum Collection. Photographic Department, The Mariners
    Museum, Newport News, VA 23606.

WASHINGTON, D.C.

Library of Congress Collection. Photoduplication Services, Library of
    Congress, Washington, D.C. 20540

National Archives Collection. Social and Economics Records Division,
    National Archives and Records Service, General Services
    Administration, 8th St. & Pennsylvania Ave., N.W., Washington,
    D.C. 20408

Smithsonian Institute. The Smithsonian Institute, Division of Trans-
    portation, Washington, D.C. 20560

WISCONSIN

Captain Edward Carus Collection. Manitowoc Maritime Museum, 809 South
    8th St., Manitowoc, WI 54200.

The Edwin Schuette Collection. Manitowoc Maritime Museum, 809 South 8th
    St., Manitowoc, WI 54220

Great Lakes Photo Collection. State Historical Society of Wisconsin,
    Madison, WI 54302.

H. H. Bennett Collection. H. H. Bennett, Photographic Studio, P. O. Box
    145, Wisconsin Dells, WI 53965.

The Herman G. Runge Collection (17,000). Milwaukee Public Library, Local
    History and Marine Room, 814 W. Wisconsin Ave., Milwaukee, WI
    53233.

Weining Marine Photography. Paul Weining Enterprises, 418 W. Oakland
    Ave., Port Washington, WI 53074.

The Welnetz Collection; Ships of the Great Lakes on Postcards. Bob
    Welnetz Studio, 3501 Custer St., Manitowoc, WI 54220.

CANADA

Great Lakes Photo Collection. Archives of Ontario, Ministry of Culture
and Recreation, 77 Grenville St., Queen's Park, Toronto, Ontario
M7A 2R9.

Great Lakes Picture Collection. Metropolitan Toronto Library, 789 Young
St., Toronto, Ontario M4W 2G8.

National Photography Collection of the Public Archives of Canada. Public
Service Section, National Photography Collection, Public Archives
Canada, 395 Wellington, Ottawa, Ontario K1A ON3.

Picture Division of the Public Archives of Canada. Custodial and Public
Service Section, Picture Division, Public Archives Canada, 395
Wellington, Ottawa, Ontario K1A ON3

10-B.   PERSONAL

CALIFORNIA

Loudon G. Wilson Collection. Loudon G. Wilson, 95 Thomas Drive, Santa
Paula, CA 93060.

MARYLAND

Jean Haviland Collection. Jean Haviland, 4129 Roland Ave., Baltimore,
MD 21211.

MICHIGAN

P. D. Ristevich Marine Photo Collection. Peter D. Ristevich, 8091
Mettetal, Detroit, MI 48228.

MINNESOTA

C. P. Labadie Pre-1900 Photos. C. Patrick Labadie, 1428 Vermillion,
Duluth, MN 55812.

Howard Weis Collection. Howard Weis, Cascade Hotel, 101 W. Third St.,
Apt. 5, Duluth, MN 55802.

WISCONSIN

Henry N. Barkhausen Collection. Henry Barkhausen, c/o Wisconsin Marine
    Historical Society, 814 W. Wisconsin Ave., Milwaukee, WI 53233.

Kenneth E. Thro Collection. Kenneth E. Thro, Marine Photographer,
    Anderson Rd., Rt. 6, Box 347, Hayward, WI 54843.

Robert Bell Collection. Robert Bell, Washington Island, WI 54246.

CANADA

Andrew Edward Young Collection - 1875-1958 (3,500). Andrew Merrilees,
    189 Old Weston Rd., Toronto, Ontario. (Deceased? Disposition of
    collection uncertain -- possibly in Canadian Archives in Ottawa.)

(Reprinted from Beeson's Marine Directory)

11-A. SPECIAL COLLECTIONS AND INDEXES

Several important special collections and indexes exist. These are
listed below. Numbers in parentheses refer to the number of items
(cards, etc.) in the file.

Burton Historical Collection, Card File of Great Lakes Ships (7,000).
    Burton Historical Collection, Detroit Public Library, 5201
    Woodward Ave., Detroit, MI 48202.

Cleveland Plain Dealer Index. 1841 to Present. Cleveland Plain Dealer,
    1801 Superior Ave., N.E., Cleveland, OH 44114.

Herman G. Runge Great Lakes Vessel File (85,000). Local History and
    Marine Room, Milwaukee Public Library, 814 W. Wisconsin Ave.,
    Milwaukee, WI 53233.

J. Norman Jensen Shipwreck Card File Collection (8,500). Chicago Histor-
    ical Society Library, Clark St. at North Ave., Chicago, IL 60614.

C. P. Labadie Vessel Index (Pre-1900 only) (30,000). C. Patrick Labadie,
    1428 Vermillion Ave., Duluth, MN 55812.

John E. Poole Vessel Card File Collection (10,000). Center for Archival
    Collections, 5th Floor, University Library, Bowling Green State
    University, Bowling Green, OH 43403.

The McDonald Card File of Great Lakes Vessels (5,000). Dossin Great Lakes
    Museum, Belle Isle, Detroit, MI 48207.

Milwaukee Sentinel Index, 1837 to 1890 (100,000). Milwaukee Public Libr-
    ary, Local History and Marine Room, 814 W. Wisconsin Ave.,
    Milwaukee, WI 53233.

New York Times Index, 1851 to Present; Quarterly, 1913-29; Annual since
    1930. New York Times, 229 W. 43rd St, New York, NY 10036.

Rollman, Wil and Baker, Cheryl. An Inventory of the Ivan H. Walton Col-
    lection. (Bentley Historical Library, University of Michigan).
    Ann Arbor, Michigan: Michigan Sea Grant Program, Publication No.
    MICHU-SG-79-604, 1979.

Society of Naval Architects and Marine Engineers. Index to Transactions, 1893-1943. New York: Society of Naval Architects and Marine Engineers, 1946.

11-B. MARINE INSURANCE

Inland Lloyds Vessel Register. Buffalo: Art-Printing Works of Matthews, Northrup & Co. (c. 1882-?). (Originally published as Lake Vessel Register, System of Classification. Buffalo: Board of Lake Underwriters (c. 1850 - c. 1880).

Mullins, Hugh A. Marine Insurance Digest. Cambridge, Maryland: Cornell Maritime Press, 1951.

Thomas, Robert. A Guide to the Value of Lake Vessels, Chiefly for the Purpose of Insurance. Buffalo: Marry, Baker & Rockwell, 1857.

11-C. MARITIME LAW

Arzt, Frederick K., comp. Navigation Laws of the United States. Washington: U. S. Department of Commerce, Bureau of Marine Inspection and Navigation, 1940.

Baer, Herbert R. Admiralty Law of the Supreme Court. 3rd ed. Charlottesville, Virginia: Mitchie Co., 1979.

Bartle, Ronald. Introduction to Shipping Law. 2nd ed. London: Sweet & Maxwell, 1963.

Dana, R. H., Jr. The Seaman's Friend. Boston: Charles C. Little & James Brown & Benjamin Loring & Co., 1841.

Marvin, William. A Treatise on the Law of Wreck and Salvage. Boston: Little, Brown, 1858.

McFee, William. The Law of the Sea. New York: J. B. Lippincott, 1950.

Norris, Martin J. The Law of Salvage. Mount Kisko, New York: Baker,
     Voorhis Co., 1958.

_____. The Law of Seamen. 3rd ed. Rochester, New York: Lawyers
     Co-operative Publishing Co., 1970.

Piper, Don Courtney. The International Law of the Great Lakes. Durham,
     North Carolina: Duke University Press, 1969.

Shepheard, H. C. "History of United States Navigation and Vessel
     Inspection Laws." Historical Transactions 1893-1943. New York:
     Society of Naval Architects and Marine Engineers, 1945.

Spencer, Herbert Ranson. A Treatise on the Law of Marine Collisions.
     Chicago: Callahan & Co., 1895.

Steadman, T. P. "The Regulation of Commerce and Navigation on the Great
     Lakes." M.A. thesis, Queens University, 1938.

Udell, G. G., comp. Laws Relating to Shipping and The Merchant Marine,
     1916-1960. Washington: U. S. Library of Congress, 1960.

U. S. Treasury Department, Bureau of Navigation. Laws of the United
     States Relating to Navigation and the Merchant Marine.
     Washington, 1895.

11-D.   BIOGRAPHIES, AUTOBIOGRAPHIES AND PERSONAL RECOLLECTIONS

Bailey, Gary L. Westcott: The First Hundred Years. Bowling Green, Ohio:
     Center for Archival Collections, Bowling Green State University,
     1979.

Bancroft, William L. "Memories of Captain Samuel Ward." Michigan
     Pioneer and Historical Collections 21 (1892): 336-337.

Bunnell, David C. The Travels and Adventures of David C. Bunnell.
Palmyra, New York: J. H. Bortles, 1831.

Diary of Soren Kristiansen: Lake Michigan Schooner Captain 1891-1893.
Iron Mountain, Michigan: Mid-Peninsula Library Cooperative, 1981.

Doner, Mary F. The Salvager, The Life of Captain Tom Reid on the Great
Lakes. Minneapolis: Ross & Haines, 1958.

Hodge, William. Captain David Wilkeson. Buffalo: Printing House of
Bigelow Brothers, 1883.

Mansfield, J. B. History of the Great Lakes. v. 2. Chicago: J. H. Beers
& Co., 1899; reprint ed., Cleveland: Freshwater Press, 1972.

Parker, John G. "Autobiography of Captain John G. Parker," Michigan
Pioneer and Historical Collections 30 (1905): 582-585.

Sanborn, Janet Coe, ed. The Autobiography of Captain Alexander McDougall.
(Also appeared serially in Inland Seas v. 23-24, 1967-68.)
Cleveland: Great Lakes Historical Society, 1968.

The Schooner LA PETITE: Journal of Captain Oscar B. Smith. (Also appeared
serially in Inland Seas.) Cleveland: Great Lakes Historical Society, 1970.

Sinclair, Captain Robert. A. Winds Over Lake Huron. Hicksville, New
York: Exposition Press, 1977.

Stewart, E. M. S. "Incidents in the Life of Mr. Eber Ward, Father of
Captain E. B. Ward." Michigan Pioneer and Historical Collections
6 (1883): 471-473.

Young, Anna G. Great Lakes Saga: The Influence of One Family in the
Development of Canadian Shipping on the Great Lakes, 1816-1931.
Toronto: Richardson, Bond & Wright, 1965.

_____. Off Watch: Today and Yesterday on the Great Lakes. Toronto:
Ryerson Press, 1957.

Cook, Alexander B. "Nineteenth Century Great Lakes Ship Portraits." Inland Seas 15 (1959): 186.

Cuthbertson, George A. Catalogue of a Selection of Water-Colour Drawings. Montreal: Marine Collection, Canada Steamship Lines, 1944.

Kuttruff, Karl. Ships of the Great Lakes, a Pictorial History. Detroit: Wayne State University Press, 1976.

Owen, Lewis. Great Lakes Shipping in the 19th Century: A Portfolio of Ten Contemporary Engravings. n.p., 1972.

Sibert, C. Thomas. "Architectural Accuracy and the Artists." Inland Seas 30 (1974): 95.

Stanton, Samuel Ward. Great Lakes Steam Vessels. American Steam Vessels Series, No. 1. Meriden, Connecticut: Meriden Gravure Co., 1962.

Young, J. W. The Rise of Lundmark Marine Painter. Chicago: Fine Arts Building, 1924.

11-F.   LOG BOOKS (Representative Material Only)

Carus Collection - Logbooks. Manitowoc Maritime Museum, Manitowoc, Wisconsin.

    BADGER STATE, 1903-04
    CHICAGO, 1895
    CITY OF LUDINGTON (Renamed GEORGIA), 1898-1903
    CORONA, 1891
    EMPIRE STATE, 1903-04
    GEORGE A. MARSH, 1882
    GEORGE BURNHAM, 1905-06
    HUNTER, 1891
    MUSKEGON, 1892
    NELLIE, 1888
    NORTH STAR, 1886
    SHEBOYGAN, 1894
    SOO CITY, 1905

Diary of Soren Kristiansen: Lake Michigan Schooner Captain 1891-1893.
    Iron Mountin, Michigan: Mid-Peninsula Library Cooperative, 1981.

Great Lakes Historical Society Log Books: Pre-1920.   Great Lakes Histor-
    ical Society, Vermilion, Ohio.

    Stmr ALEXIS W. THOMPASON (was SOCAPA), 1908-09
    Stmr AURORA, 1896
    Stmr AUSTRALIA, 1902, 1908-13
    Stmr CALEDONIA, 1898, 1901-02
    Stmr E. L. WALLACE, 1914
    Stmr ERWIN L. FISHER, 1912, April 15-December 10, 1915
    FIREBOAT, November 1886-June 1887
    FIREBOAT #15, January 1892-September 1892, December 1895, 1896
    Stmr GEORGE STONE, 1908
    Stmr JAMES LAUGHLIN, 1908-09
    Stmr KEARSARGE, 1900-03
    Stmr LAUGLIN, 1910
    Stmr M. A. BRADLEY, 1912-13
    Stmr NORWALK, 1895
    Stmr RHODES, 1906
    Stmr SOCAPA, 1907
    Sch THOMAS GAWN, May 1878-June 1880, May 1881-October 1881
    Sch W. G. LYONS, April 1871-November 1872
    Stmr W. L. WETMORE, 1895
    Stmr WILSON, 1911

The Neff Collection: Great Lakes Account Ledger Books of the Samuel
    Neff & Sons Co. Milwaukee Public Library, Milwaukee, Wisconsin.

    Stmr ADELLA SHORES, 1900-03
    Stmr CHARLES S. NEFF, 1905-06
    Sch CONNELLY BROTHERS, 1915
    Stmr EDWIN S. TICE, 1900
    Stmr KALKASKA, 1918-20
    Bge LIBERTY, 1918-20
    Stmr LUCY NEFF, 1902
    Stmr MARION, 1900-02
    Stmr MINNIE E. KELTON, 1900-03
    Bge MYSTIC M. ROSS, 1890
    Bge O. J. HALE, 1900
    Stmr VENEZUELA, 1818-20

The Schooner LA PETITE: Journal of Captain Oscar B. Smith. Cleveland:
    Great Lakes Historical Society, reprint ed., 1970.

A Spirit Revelation from the Great Deep; or a Cargo of Old Liquors on the Bottom of Lake Erie and How to Find It. Chicago: Favorite Wrecking Co. (c. 1876). (Schooner FAVORITE.)

Burgess, Robert F. They Found Treasure. New York: Dodd, Mead & Co., 1977.

Marx, Robert F. Spanish Treasure in Florida Waters: A Billion Dollar Graveyard. Boston: Mariners Press, 1979.

Potter, John S., Jr., and Nesmith, R. T. Treasure - How and Where to Find It, "The Great Lakes." New York: Arco Publishing Co., 1968.

Potter, John S., Jr. The Treasure Diver's Guide. New York: Doubleday Co., 1972.

Rieseberg, Lt. Harry E., and Mikalow, A. Fell's Guide to Sunken Treasure Ships of the World. New York: Frederick Fell Publishing Co., 1965.

Rieseberg, Lt. Harry E. Fell's Complete Guide to Buried Treasure, Land and Sea. New York: Frederick Fell Publishing Co., 1967.

Treasure Ships of the Great Lakes. Detroit: Maritime Research & Publishing Co., 1981.

11-H.   ENVIRONMENTAL CONTROL AND LIMNOLOGY

Barry, James P. The Fate of the Lakes: A Portrait of the Great Lakes. Grand Rapids, Michigan: Baker Book House, 1972.

Great Lakes Basin Commission. Annual Report. Ann Arbor, Michigan: Great Lakes Basin Commission, 1976 to present.

Great Lakes Commssion. Great Lakes Newsletter (Monthly). Ann Arbor, Michigan: Institute of Science and Technology, 1956 to present.

International Joint Commission. The Great Lakes Notebook (Monthly). Windsor, Ontario: Great Lakes Regional Office Information Services.

Michigan Department of Natural Resources. Highlights of Water Quality
and Pollution Control in Michigan. Lansing, Michigan: Comprehensive Studies Section, Environmental Services Division, 1981.

Steinhacker, Charles, photographer. Superior: Portrait of a Living Lake,
by Arno Karlan, ed. 2nd ed. New York: Harper & Row, 1970.

U. S. Department of Commerce, National Oceanic and Atmospheric Administration, National Ocean Survey. Great Lakes Water Levels, 1860-
1970. Detroit: Lake Survey Center, 1971.

Weimer, Linda, et al. Our Great Lakes, Booklet. Madison: University of
Wisconsin Sea Grant College Program, 1973.

11-I.   SALVAGE, WRECKING AND UNDERWATER ARCHAEOLOGY

Bass, Geroge F., ed. A History of Seafaring Based on Underwater Archaeology. New York: Walker & Co., 1972.

Burgess, Robert F. Man, 12,000 Years Under the Sea: A Story of Underwater Archaeology. New York: Dodd, Mead & Co., 1980.

Deep Sea Diving School, U. S. Naval Weapons Plant. Ship Salvage Notes.
Washington: Deep Sea Diving School, U. S. Naval Weapons Plant,
1960.

Doner, Mary F. The Salvager, the Life of Captain Tom Reid on the Great
Lakes. Minneapolis: Ross & Haines, 1958.

Dugan, James. World Beneath the Sea. Washington: National Geographic
Society, 1967.

Green, John B. Diving With and Without Armor. Buffalo: Faxon's Steam
Power Press Co., 1859.

Jenney, Jim. In Search of Shipwrecks. Cranbury, New Jersey: A. S. Barnes
& Co., 1980.

Johnson, R. F. The ROYAL GEORGE. London: Charles Knight & Co., 1971.

Kennaugh, W. E. and Company. Proposal to the Marine Insurance Companies
      of the City of Chicago Concerning the Recovery of Wrecked Vessels.
      Washington: W. E. Kennaugh & Co., 1860.

Limburg, Peter R., and Sweeney, James B. Vessels for Underwater Explora-
      tion. New York: Crown Publishers, 1973.

Marx, Robert F. They Dared the Deep: A History of Diving. Cleveland:
      World Publishing Co., 1967.

Meier, Frank. Fathoms Below. New York: E. P. Dutton & Co., 1943.

The Mystery Ship From 19 Fathoms. AuTrain, Michigan: Avery Color Studios,
      1974. (The ALVIN CLARK.)

New York State, Office of State History. Diving Into History: A Manual
      of Underwater Archaeology for Divers in New York State. New York,
      New York State, Office of State History, 1969.

Petersen, Mendel. History Under the Sea, a Handbook for Underwater
      Exploration. Alexandria, Virginia: By the Author, 1973.

Shepard, Birse. Lore of the Wreckers. Boston: Beacon Press, 1961.

Smith, F. Hopkinson. Caleb West, Master Diver. New York: Charles
      Scribner's Sons, 1908.

_____. Captain Thomas A. Scott, Master Diver. Boston: American Unitar-
      ian Association, 1908.

Stabelfeldt, Kimm A. Wreck Diver's Handbook. Milwaukee: Rowe Publica-
      tions, 1981.

The Underwater Demolition Team Handbook. Boulder, Colorado: Paladin
      Press, 1965.

Wheeler, Robert C. Q., Kenyon, Walter A., Woolworth, Alan R., and Birk, Douglas A. Voices from the Rapids: An Underwater Search for Artifacts from the Fur Trade, 1960-73. St. Paul, Minnesota: Minnesota Historical Society, 1975.

Wilkes, Bill S. Nautical Archaeology: A Handbook for Skin Divers. New York: Stein & Day, 1971.

Young, Desmond. The Man in the Helmet. n.p. (c.1855).

Young, Desmond. Ships Ashore; Adventures in Salvage. London: J. Cape, 1932.

11-J.   MISCELLANEOUS

Belford, Richard A. The Ragged Rimes of a Great Lakes Steamboat Man. Cleveland: By the Author, 1974.

Falconer, William. The Shipwreck, a Poem. London: T. Bensley, 1804.

Great Lakes Stack Charts. Cleveland: Freshwater Press, 1982.

Gourlay, Jay. The Great Lakes Triangle. Greenwich, Conneticut: Fawcett, 1977.

Horton, John L. Great Lakes Seamanship. Vermilion, Ohio: n.p., 1942.

Jaussi, Laureen R., and Chaston, Gloria D. Fundamentals of Genealogical Research. Salt Lake City, Utah: Desert Book Co., 1977. (Chapter 8 contains an excellent practical description on how to use a library.)

Johnson, Robert C. "Ballads of Disasters on the Great Lakes." New York Folklore Quarterly (Spring 1949).

Lightfoot, Gordon. "The Wreck of the EDMOND FITZGERALD." (Song) Published by Moose Music Ltd, 1976. Available on the Lightfoot Album Summertime Dream. Warner Bros. Records, Burbank, California, 1976.

Preece, Floren Stocks, and Preece, Phyllis Pastore. <u>Handy Guide to</u>
<u>English Genealogical Records</u>. Logan, Utah: Everton Publishers,
1972. (See page 10 ff for simplified approach and references on
reading handwriting in Old English records.)

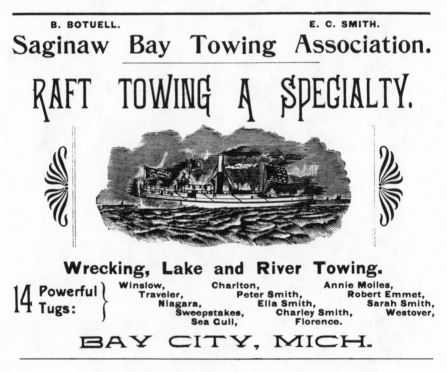

12-A. *LIBRARIES AND DEPOSITORIES OF GREAT LAKES MARITIME HISTORY*

CONNECTICUT

G. W. Blunt White Library. Mystic Seaport, Greenmanville Ave., Mystic,
     CT 06355

ILLINOIS

Chicago Historical Society Library. J. Norman Jensen Collection. Clark
     St. at North Ave., Chicago, IL 60614.

Chicago Public Library. 78 E. Washington St., Chicago, IL 60614

National Archives Regional Records Service Center, Chicago Branch. 7358
     South Pulaski Rd., Chicago, IL 60629

MARYLAND

Jean Haviland Library (Private Collection). 4129 Roland Ave., Baltimore,
     MD 21211.

The Steamship Historical Society of America Library, University of
     Baltimore Library, 1420 Maryland Ave., Baltimore, MD 21201.

MICHIGAN

Bayliss Public Library. Sault Ste. Marie, MI 49783

Detroit Public Library. Burton Historical Collection, 5201 Woodward Ave.,
     Detroit, MI 48202.

Henry Ford Centennial Library, 16301 Michigan Ave., Dearborn, MI 48126.

J. M. Longyear Research Library. Marquette County Historical Society,
     213 North Front St., Marquette, MI 49855.

Michigan Technological University Library. Houghton, MI 49931.

Port Huron Public Library. 219 McMorran, Port Huron, MI 48060.

Purdy Library. Wayne State University, 5210 Gunnen Mall, Detroit, MI
    48202.

St. Clair County Library. W. L. Jenks Historical Collection, 210
    McMorran, Port Huron, MI 48060.

State of Michigan Library Services. 735 E. Michigan Ave., Lansing, MI
    48909.

University of Michigan Library. Ann Arbor, MI 48104.

MINNESOTA

Canal Park Museum Library. U. S. Army Corps of Engineers, Duluth, MN
    55802.

NEW YORK

Buffalo and Erie County Historical Society Library. 25 Nottingham Court,
    Buffalo, NY 14216.

Buffalo and Erie County Public Library. Lafayette Square, Buffalo, NY
    14203.

New York Historical Society Library. 170 Central Park West, New York, NY
    10024.

New York Public Library. General Research and Humanities Division, 42nd
    St. & 5th Ave., New York, NY 10018.

Stephen B. Luce Library. Maritime College, State University of New York,
    Bronx, NY 10465.

OHIO

Center for Archival Collections. Bowling Green State University, 5th
    Floor Library, Bowling Green, OH 43403.

Clarence Metcalfe Library. Great Lakes Historical Society, 480 Main St.,
    Vermilion, OH 44089.

Cleveland Public Library. 325 Superior, Cleveland, OH 44114.

Great Lakes Research (Private Collection). Walter Remick, 6103 Dennison
    Ave., Cleveland, OH 44102.

Rutherford B. Hayes Library. Great Lakes Marine Collection, 1337 Hayes
    Ave., Fremont, OH 43420.

WASHINGTON, D.C.

Library of Congress. Washington, D.C. 20542

National Archives and Records Service. (GSA), Washington, D.C. 20408.

Smithsonian Institute. Transportation Division, Washington, D.C. 20560.

WISCONSIN

Milwaukee Public Library. Local History and Marine Room, 814 W. Wiscon-
    son, Milwaukee, WI 53233.

CANADA

Archives of Ontario. Ministry of Culture and Recreation, 77 Grenville
    St., Queen's Park, Toronto, Ontario M7A 2R9.

Metropolitan Toronto Library. 789 Young St., Toronto, Ontaro M4W 2G8.

Trade and Communications Records. Federal Archives Division, Public
    Archives of Canada, 395 Wellington St., Ottawa, Ontario K1A ON3.

MICHIGAN

Bay County Historical Society. 1700 Center Ave., Bay City, MI 48706.

Delta County Historical Society. South 2nd St., Ludington Park,
Escanaba, MI 49829.

Great Lakes Maritime Institute. 100 The Strand, Belle Isle, Detroit, MI
48207.

Great Lakes Shipwreck Historical Society, Route 2, Box 279-A, Sault Ste.
Marie, MI 49783

The Lake Huron Lore Marine Society. Museum of Arts and History, 1115 6th
St., Port Huron, MI 48060.

Marine Historical Society of Detroit. 4190 Green Dr., Harsens Island, MI
48028

Marquette County Historical Society. 213 North Front St., Marquette, MI
49855.

The Michilimackinac Historical Society. St. Ignace, MI 49781.

Saginaw Bay Marine Historical Society. 8750 E. Burt Rd., Birch Run, MI
48414.

MINNESOTA

The Lake Superior Marine Museum Association. Canal Park, Duluth, MN 55802

Minnesota Historical Society. Split Rock Lighthouse, E. Star Route, Two
Harbors, MN 55616

St. Louis County Historical Society. 506 W. Michigan St., Duluth, MN
55616

NEW YORK

Buffalo and Erie County Historical Society. 25 Nottingham Court,
      Buffalo, NY 14216.

New York Historical Society. 170 Central Park West, New York, NY 10024.

OHIO

The Canal Society of Ohio. 550 Copley Rd., Akron, OH 44320.

The Great Lakes Historical Society. 480 Main St., Vermilion, OH 44089.

Ross County Historical Society. 45 West Fifth St., Chillicothe, OH 45601.

The Western Lake Erie Historical Society. 5902 Swan Creek Dr., Toledo,
      OH 43614.

Western Reserve Historical Society. 10825 East Blvd., Cleveland, OH 44106.

RHODE ISLAND

Steamship Historical Society of America, Inc. 170 Westminster St., Room
      1103, Providence, RI 02903.

WISCONSIN

Head of the Lakes Maritime Society. P. O. Box 178, Superior, WI 54880.

Manitowoc Marine Historical Society. 809 S. 8th St., Manitowoc, WI 54220.

Wisconsin Marine Historical Society. 814 W. Wisconsin Ave., Milwaukee, WI
      53233.

CANADA

St. Mary's River Marine Society. Saulte Ste. Marie, Ontario.

Thunder Bay Historical Society. 219 South May St., Thunder Bay, Ontario.

Toronto Marine Historical Society. Toronto, Ontario.

Wellands Canals Preservation Association. Box 1224. St. Catherines, Ontario L2R 7A7.

World Ship Society. Toronto, Ontario.

12-C.   GREAT LAKES MARITIME MUSEUMS

INDIANA

The Old Lighthouse. Michigan City, IN 46360.

MICHIGAN

Great Lakes Shipwreck Memorial Museum. Whitefish Point Lighthouse, White-fish Point, MI 49798. (To be opened in 1983.)

Grosse Isle Historical Museum. E. River Drive & Parkway. Grosse Isle, MI 48138.

Jesse D. Besser Museum. 491 Johnson St., Alpena, MI 49707.

Huron City Coast Guard Station. The Old Point Aux Barques Station, Huron City, MI 48467.

Huron Lightship. Black River, Port Huron, MI 48060.

Lake Michigan Maritime Museum. Dyckman Ave., South Haven, MI 49090.

Mackinac Maritime Museum. Mackinaw City, MI 49701.

Manistee County Historical Museum. 425 River St., Manistee, MI 49660.

Marine Museum on Beaver Island. St. James, MI 49782.

Marquette Marine Museum. 501 East Arch, Marquette, MI 49855.

Mason County Museum. Ludington, MI 49431.

Michigan Historical Museum. 208 N. Capitol Ave., Lansing, MI 48918.

Museum of Arts and History. 1115 6th St., Port Huron, MI 48060.

Museum of the Great Lakes. 1700 Center Ave., Bay City, MI 48706.

Mystery Ship Seaport. 13th St. in River Park, Menominee, MI 49858.

Northwest Michigan Maritime Museum. 324 Main St., Frankfort, MI 49635.

The Old Lighthouse. Presque Isle Harbor, Alpena, MI 49707.

Pilot House Museum. "Nautical City" Rogers City, MI 49779.

Rose Hawley Museum. 305 E. Filer St., Ludington, MI 49431.

Sleeping Bear Dunes National Lakeshore. Frederickson Collection, Empire,
       MI 49630.

S. S. KEEWATIN Marne Museum. Box 511, Douglas, MI 49406.

S. S. VALLEY CAMP Marine Museum. P.O. Box 1688, Port Adventure, Saulte
       Ste. Marie, MI 49783.

Teysen's Talking Bear Museum. 416 South Huron Ave., Mackinaw City, MI
       49701.

The WELCOME. Reconstructed 1775 Wooden Sloop, Mackinaw City Marina,
       Mackinaw City, MI 49701.

MINNESOTA

Canal Park Marine Museum. U. S. Army Corps of Engineers, Duluth, MN 55802

Split Rock Light Station. E. Star Rt., Box 125, Two Harbors, MN 55616.

NEW YORK

New York State Maritime Museum. South & Fulton Streets, New York, NY 1000

U.S.S. LITTLE ROCK. A World War II Cruiser, Naval and Servicemen's Park,
    Buffalo, NY 14240.

OHIO

Campus Martius Museum. 601 Second St., Marietta, OH 45750.

Fairport Harbor Marine Museum. 129 Second St., Fairport, OH 44077.

Great Lakes Historical Museum. 480 Main St., Vermilion, OH 44089.

U.S.S. COD. World War II Submarine, The Great Lakes Historical Society,
    Cleveland Lakefront, Cleveland, OH 44101.

Remick Great Lakes Marine Collection. 6103 Dennison, Cleveland, OH 44102.

PENNSYLVANIA

Brig NIAGARA. McAllister's Marina, Erie, PA 16512

Erie Historical Museum. 356 W. Sixth Ave., Erie, PA 16512. (Battle of
    Lake Erie Exhibit.)

VIRGINIA

Mariner's Museum. Museum Drive, Newport News, VA 23606.

WISCONSIN

The Door County Maritime Museum. Gills Rock, Ellison Bay, WI 54210
     (Also in Sturgeon Bay, WI 54235.)

Head of the Lakes Maritime Museum. S. S. METEOR (Retired 1896 Whaleback).
     Barkers Island, Box 178, Superior, WI 54880.

Living Lakes Museum. Algoma, WI 54201.

Manitowoc Maritime Museum. 809 S. 8th St., Manitowoc, WI 54220.

Milwaukee Public Library. Local History and Marine Room, 814 W. Wisconsin
     Ave., Milwaukee, WI 53233.

Neville Public Musuem. 129 S. Hefferson St., Green Bay, WI 54305.

The Sunken Treasures Maritime Museum. P. O. Box 64, Port Washington, WI
     53074.

CANADA

The Bruce County Museum. South Hampton, Ontario.

Collingwood Museum. St. Paul Street, Collingwood, Ontario.

Historic Naval and Military Establishment. Penetanguishene, Ontario.

HMS. HAIDA (Canadian Destroyer). Lakeshore Blvd, Toronto, Ontario.

HMS. TECUMSETH. Penetanguishene, Ontario.

Kanawa International Museum of Canoes. Minden, Ontario.

Maitland County Marine Museum. Goderich, Ontario.

Marine Museum of the Great Lakes at Kingston. 55 Ontario St., Kingston,
     Ontario.

Marine Museum of Upper Canada. Exhibition Park, Toronto, Ontario.

Mariners' Memorial Lighthouse Park. County Roads 9 and 13, South Bay,
        Ontario.

Mississaugi Strait Lighthouse Museum. Meldrum Bay, Ontario.

Museum/Passenger Auto-Ferry. Manitoulin Island, Manitowaning, Ontario.

Museum of the Upper Lakes. Nancy Island, Wasaga Beach, Ontario.

Museum Ship NORGOMA. Sault Ste. Marie, Ontario.

Peterborough Centennial Museum and Archives and Museum of the Trent
        System Waterway. Peterborough, Ontario.

Pilot House Museum. Corunna, Ontario.

Pilot House Museum. 18th St. Clair Parkway, Sarnia, Ontario.

Port Colborne Historical and Marine Museum. Port Colborne, Ontario.

Port Dover Harbour Museum. Port Dover, Ontario.

S. S. SEGWUN Museum. Gravenhurst, Ontario.

Schooner MINK. Old Fort William, Thunder Bay, Ontario.

St. Catharines Historical Museum. St. Catharines, Ontario.

St. Edmunds Township Museum. Tobermory, Ontario.

Thunder Bay Historical Society Museum. 219 South May St., Thunder Bay,
        Ontario.

Voyageur Canoe Exhibit. Mattawa, Ontario

Welland Historical Museum. Welland, Ontario.

BOOKS ABOUT MUSEUMS

Aymar, Brandt. A Pictorial Treasury of the Marine Museums of the World.
New York: Crown Publishers, 1967.

Historical Musuems in Michigan: A Visitor's Guide. Pamphlet. Ann Arbor,
Michigan: Historical Society of Michigan, 1978.

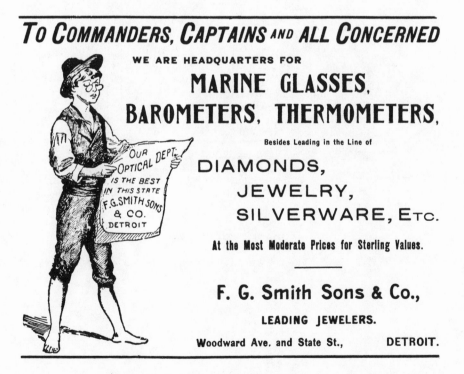

(Reprinted from Beeson's Marine Directory)

FORE-AND-AFT THREE-MASTED SCHOONER

(Reprinted from Merchant Vessels)

Since the printing press was invented in the mid-fifteenth century, there have been over 30,000,000 books printed in the world. The average large library may have holdings of three to four million volumes or about 10% of the world's published literature. Needless to say, ferreting out and identifying all of the works pertinent to a narrow scope subject such as Great Lakes maritime history can indeed be a monumental task. The authors are not so naive as to believe that this bibliography completely accomplishes the above goal. Yet we do believe it captures in organized form the majority of the extant literature in book form on our chosen subject. Certainly, bibliographical universality is most nearly achieved by the card catalogs of the larger libraries of the world. For an over-view of published material on general maritime history, we strongly recommend the bibliography by Robert G. Albion (Section 1-B).

The majority of the citations are books or booklets. Neverthe-less, material from journals and serials have been included where we have felt it is important, i.e., where the subject matter has not been adequately covered in book form (examples are Alexander Meakin's "History of the Great Lakes Towing Company" which, to our knowledge, has not been published in book form but which appeared serially in *Inland Seas*). We also make no apology for listing Tom Odle's thesis on the American grain trade on the Lakes (Section 2-C-1) as appearing serially in *Inland Seas*. Obviously it is readily available on microfilm but we find it much less work to read it in *Inland Seas*. Section 12 is of course not bibliogra-phic material but rather a guide to libraires, socieites and musuems concerned with Great Lakes maritime history.

In several sections, citations are not limited to the Great Lakes (see Section 3-A as an example). Yet we believe some knowledge of mari-time history outside of the bounds of the Great Lakes is essential to developing an overall perspective of Great Lakes maritime history (after all, the British "Merchant Shipping Act of 1854" introducing the Moorsom tonnage system was not invented for the Great Lakes but it is important to have some knowledge of this relative to the BOM system if one is to

research U. S. Great Lakes vessels built prior to 1864 which survived
past 1865).

In the world of professional bibliography, the word "incunabula"
is usually reserved to categorize books printed before 1501 A.D. However, Webster also allows that it is "a work of art or of human industry
of an early epoch." In the case of Great Lakes maritime history, we
would define "incunabula" as material published prior to about 1865.
It was around this time that the new tonnage system, the official numbering system, "Merchant Vessels," etc., were introduced, as well as the
major restructuring and revitalization of government agencies responsible
for various aspects of transportation on the Great Lakes took place.
Consequently, the amount of printed material of historical significance
grew rapidly after the end of the Civil War. Even so, it is often
difficult to determine the existence and location of material prior to
1900. Thus, we have placed appreciable emphasis on identifying and
listing classical works published prior to 1900. Note also that this
bibliography is limited almost exclusively to citations which are
written in the English language.

The opening section on Reference Works includes a select list of
basic research tools (Section 1-A). This was done because the prepond-
erence of people who are doing Great Lakes maritime historical research,
or who intend to, are not professional historians and their skills in
research and library usage may be "rusty." We would particularly recommend the books by Cheney and Downs for those who desire to improve their
library research skills. The value of being conversant with reference
sources cannot be overemphasized.

In this first edition, we have not tried to provide the reader
with any indices of "selectively" of works listed in a given subject
area. Moreover, although some citations are annotated, the majority
are not. Additionally, many of the pre-1900 listings can often only be
found in a very limited number of libraries or archives. Thus, the

reader often may be faced with a considerable task in locating a library which actually has a copy of a listed citation. We suggest the reader consult the National Union Catalogs (listed in Section 1-D) as library locations are shown using the standard symbols of the American Library Association or the Library of Congress.

This bibliography, although it includes appreciable Canadian material, is undoubtedly stronger in the area of U. S. publications. The bibliography by Nobles *et al* (Section 1-B), though unpublished, contains a wealth of additional information on Canadian sources. Other areas receiving little or no coverage include manuscripts, log books, ship plans and other ephemeral material. Such subjects are generally outside the scope of this publication. As previously stated, this bibliography was not intended to include individual entries from periodicals, serials and journals. We suggest you consult the Readers' Guide to Periodical Literature listed in Section 1-D for listings of this sort. It is our intention that several of the shortcomings mentioned above will be addressed in future editions.

Within reason the style recommendations of Kate Turabian in the fourth edition of her work entiteld "A Manual for Writers" (University of Chicago Press, 1973) have been followed. Violations of the rules promulgated in Ms. Turabian's manual have resulted from our experience in working the card catalogs of scores of libraries. The primary objective is to provide a bibliography which is pragmatic in its approach to citing (and eventually locating) information.

Although this Appendix is meant to provide "perspective," it is not intended as a guide to the usage of this bibliography. This publication remains a bibliography, i.e., a description and systemization of publications on Great Lakes maritime history. Currently we are working on a "How To" book which will serve as an interpretative guide to the logical utilization of this bibliography. Such a guide, with its concomitant research methodology, is planned for publication in the near future.

BRIG

(Reprinted from Merchant Vessels)

★ LOSING THE STRUGGLE ★
by Edward Pusick

AN INVITATION TO OUR READERS

A work of this sort is never complete or free from error. We would appreciate our readers bringing both the errors and oversights, as well as new citations, etc., to our attention. In the case of errors, please provide a full citation for the correct version. For additions, please provide both the full citation, a brief annotation of the contents and the recommended section number in which it should be listed. Forward all information to Seajay Publications, P. O. Box 2176, Dearborn MI 48123. Worthy contributions will be duly acknowledged in future editions. Thank you.

BARK

(Reprinted from Merchant Vessels)